Happy Trails!
To Nancy Sell and family,
Thank you!

Pioneer Cowboy

Bill Helm

The Life and Gold Stories of Cowboy Bill Helm

Written and Compiled
by
Billie Helm

Billie

Copyright © 2015 Billie Helm

All rights reserved.

ISBN–10: 1505306116
ISBN-13: 978-1505306118

Dedication

This book is dedicated to all of the people that have been part of my life. In my early years and as I grew up my dad George Helm was my friend, partner, and an example to follow.

I would also like to dedicate this book to the Walt Randall family. I started my cowboy life on their ranch in Bloody Basin at the age of 14 in 1943. They had faith in me and gave me a chance to prove my self-worth.

This book needs to also be dedicated to the many friends I have had throughout my life. Among them are Art Hargrave, Clint Self, Bobby Parker, and John (Jackie) Newberry. These people stood by me through thick and thin.

Furthermore, I dedicate this book to Janie Helm. She provided much encouragement when I desperately needed it.

Additionally, I dedicate this book to the young people that I had a chance to know and help over the years both as a sheriff and a friend.

It is also important that I also dedicate this book of my life to my children Billy, Randy, Judy, and Marie. I love them very much and always did my best to provide for them no matter what. I am proud of the God trusting men and women they have become. For this reason they are survivors as I feel this cowboy is.

Acknowledgements

I acknowledge and thank my wife Billie for her dedication in putting this book together of my experiences as I lived my life. I realize it has taken many hours, days, and years to make it the book that it is.

I also thank writer Allen Kelley of Red Rock Writers for assisting her with editing, proofreading, and design. I also want to thank Debbie Pearson for all she did to finalize this book of my life.

Table of Contents

Introduction.. i

Chapter 1 - Bill's Early Years in Fossil Creek, Irving, and Childs.................................... 1

Chapter 2 - Bill's Cowboy Life 25

Chapter 3 - Horse Camp 67

Chapter 4 - Hydroelectric Power Plants 93

Chapter 5 - Cattle Drives – and Bill's Horses 113

Chapter 6 - Bill's Gold Stories 123

Chapter 7 - House Builder and Trucker 135

Chapter 8 - Irving Power Plant Reunion 145

Chapter 9 - Bill as Sheriff and Lawman 151

Chapter 10 - Bill and Billie Family and Friends 159

References 181

Introduction

Charles William (Bill) Helm Sr. (1929)
Arizona Cowboy

Pioneer Cowboy Bill Helm and Smoke

Bloody Basin Introduction

Bloody Basin is a large part of Bill's life and most of the tales and stories in this book are woven around the "Bloody Basin" and "Fossil Creek" areas in Arizona.

Bloody Basin with its ancient Indian ruins, desert vegetation, wildlife, and cattle, is located in central Arizona. Bloody Basin is a big, rough, primitive, wild, mountain-rimmed stretch of country 100 miles north of Phoenix and

30 miles west of Payson. Frowning down on Bloody Basin is flat-topped Skeleton Ridge, once a natural fortress. The United States Cavalry wiped out a small band of Apaches during the last of the Indian battles in 1873. One of the last skirmishes was made on Skeleton Ridge and that's where the Indians' bones whitened and turned to dust. (Schubert, 1958)

Skeleton Ridge

According to John Bourke, author of "On the Border with Crook," in March of 1873 near Wickenburg, Arizona, a large band of Tonto Apaches attacked a small group of young prospectors who had recently arrived from England.

The Apaches tied two of the prospectors to a cactus and filled them with arrows. They also robbed and killed the Englishmen, stole or killed the cattle and horses, and struck out across the Bradshaw Mountains. When Capt. George M. Randall of the 23rd Infantry found out about it, the Apaches already had a twenty-four hour head start on them.

After the raid and killings, the Apaches headed for Turret Peak (see picture). One of Randall's Indian scouts told him that the Apaches would feel safe there because they fancied that no enemy would dare follow them to their sacred place.

Turret Peak

On top of Turret Peak, one can see for miles in every direction. Capt. Randall and his men had to hide out during the day and get closer to the peak at night. When the Infantry finally arrived at the foot of the Peak at night, Capt. Randall made his men crawl up the face of the mountain slowly on their hands and knees.

He wanted to make sure they didn't make any noise as a result of the rattling of stones that could be heard by the Apaches. After midnight, Capt. Randall and his men reached the top of the Peak where the Apaches were camped with their campfires still burning.

Capt. Randall waited till daybreak and then led the charge. Many of the panic-stricken Apaches ran and jumped off the ledge to their deaths.

Soldiers killed many more on the Peak; the rest of them surrendered. This was the last battle fought by the Apaches as a Tribe. This Battle at Turret Peak specifically resulted in the name "Bloody Basin" being given to this locale.

Bloody Basin Road

There were no roads in the early days. Even the road that exists now is very narrow, washboard, rocky, and just gets worse as one drivers closer to the Verde River.

Bloody Basin is still plenty wild and the men who lived there in the past are characters right out of the "Old Wild West".

Biscuit Butte in Bloody Basin

Indian Paint Brush and Metate

Metate and Mano (below) are used for grinding corn into flour by ancient Indians

Metate

Ed Note: While varying in specific morphology, metates adhere to a common shape. They typically consist of large stones with a smooth depression or bowl worn into the upper surface. The bowl is formed by the continual and long-term grinding of materials using a smooth hand-held stone (known as a mano). This action consists of a horizontal grinding motion that differs from the vertical crushing motion used in a mortar and pestle. The depth of the bowl varies, though they are typically not deeper than those of a mortar; deeper Metate bowls indicate either a longer period of use or greater degree of activity (i.e., economic specialization). Quoted from **Wikipedia**

Bloody Basin Sign
Great Western Trail – Tonto National Forest

Chapter 1
Bill's Early Years
in Fossil Creek, Irving, and Childs

My father George Henry Helm was born in Mayer, Arizona on August 3, 1897 and his father Eligh Helm was born on June 7, 1826. My Grandfather Eligh Helm came to Arizona in the late 1860's shortly after the new Arizona Territory was established.

George Henry Helm – Bill's Father

He homesteaded on the Big Bug Creek near Mayer and soon sent for my grandmother Jessica whom he had left in Texas. The family then permanently settled in Arizona. He died at Big Bug, Arizona on August 23, 1908.

My family was one of the first settlers of the Big Bug area. I have an older brother named George Edward who was born in 1927 in Big Bug. I was born Charles William Helm in Winkelman, Arizona, June 10, 1929, and raised in the Fossil Creek/Childs/Irving/Bloody Basin/Camp Verde area. I was one month old when my family came back to this area. Fossil Creek runs through Irving, where my father began working at the Power Plant for the second time.

I also have a sister named Barbara Ellen who was born in Cottonwood, Arizona in 1933. Camp Verde is one of the closest towns to Cottonwood, and it is around 15 miles south of Cottonwood.

Bill's Aunt Nellie (Helm) Goodwin

Nellie and her husband Walter Goodwin lived in Jerome Arizona down in the "gulch". They raised chickens and sold eggs to the miners' families. At that time, Jerome was a thriving copper mining town.

Bill's Aunt Lela Helm

When she was thirteen or fourteen years old, she was rabbit hunting with Bill's Dad George one day. She leaned her 10-gauge muzzleloader shotgun against the barbed wire fence. She was doing this while she held the wires apart so he could get through it. Her gun fell down and her right arm was hit by the blast. They did manage to get her back home alive. A Doctor Looney came out of Prescott in his buckboard wagon but he couldn't save her arm.

Lela later married and moved to California. She and her husband raised and sold avocados. Every Christmas, Bill's mother would get a lug (double layered cartons) of avocados from them.

Standing in back row from left to right are Aunt Verne Douglas, Martha Ellen Foster (mother), Aunt Thelma Foster (next to mother on right), Aunt Maggie Sessions (far right)
Front row: Floy Fay Foster (Bill's mother) on left, Aunt Lizzie Zellner (middle of picture)

Floy Fay's Parents and Bill's Grandparents Joseph (Joe) and Martha Ellen Foster

Joseph and Martha Ellen Foster

Bill's Dad's 1924 Hupmobile

Bill's mother complained because the car had no windows or blinds. When it rained, everyone got wet.

George Henry Helm holding Bill Helm. George Edward Helm sitting on rocks. Note: Indians walking on flume cover in background.

Bill's mother Floy Fay Helm with Bill and Bill's sister Barbara

George and Barbara Ellen with mother Floy Fay Helm taken at Irving Power Plant

NOTE: – Bill's Great Grandmother (Cherokee Indian) Jenny Helm's Healing Remedies:

Chest congestion - warm cow patty on chest –

Or - Skunk oil (made from boiled down skunk fat) - compared to our Vicks ointment today.

Bill's mother Floy Fay Helm - 1946

The company provided housing for the employees and schooling for their children

One room school house near Irving Power Plant
Note: Bill Helm went to school in this one room school house through the 8th Grade.

Childs-Irving one-room school house foundation as it is today

School Days in one room schoolhouse

Fossil Creek School at Irving - Taken in 1935

School Teacher: Miss Burris

Back Row: JC Burris, George Helm, Floyd Lewis
Third Row: Donny Robertson, Frank Godard, Billy Godard
Second Row: Richard Lewis, Charles (Bill) Helm, Glen Lewis, Maxine Womack
Front Row: Verdan Robertson, Virginia Womack, Betty Womack, Mary Ellen Garrison, Lois Garrison

The children had to walk on the flume cover on their way to school

There were about 14 kids in the school with classes from kindergarten to eighth grade being held at the same time together. There was a school bus that transported kids from Childs and the surrounding areas to Irving. They then had to walk on the flume cover the rest of the way to the school. None of the children ever fell into the flume.

When the weather was cold, parents would drive their kids to school in their pickups.

**Sunday School – held in one room school house
Bill Helm in back row on left**

The Franklin Godard kids lived close enough to ride their horses to school. They tied them to trees next to the school all day and rode them back home when school was out. They lived on the Fossil Creek road about 2 miles from the Irving Power Plant.

Their mailbox was a 5-gallon can sitting on a rock post. This mailbox is still standing next to the road near the gate in front of their house. Franklin Godard also ran a gas station that was located between his home and the Irving Power Plant. George Edward Helm worked at the station for many years.

The Godards also had a nice orchard with apple, fig, peach and other fruit trees. Bill Helm ate so many figs one time that he became very sick.

Many years later, Clinton Winters bought the lumber from the old school house after it was torn down and he then built a house in Bridgeport, Arizona.

Bill and the children from other families had to provide their own entertainment. They swam and fished in **Fossil Creek**.

Fossil Springs Swimming Hole

Bill, George, and Barbara Ellen with rabbit dinner.

Bill and George on a horse held by Bob Peach

Bill and George on a road grader at Cherry, AZ

Bill's sister - Barbara Ellen Helm - 9 years old

Bill and his first horse at age nine in 1938

In those days there was a lot of open country to ride in.

When Bill was 8 years old his mother and father separated. His mother moved to Phoenix with his sister Barbara and George and Bill stayed with their father in Irving.

When his brother George was about 15 he moved to Camp Verde to live with their Aunt Vernie and Uncle Volley Douglas to attend school. He had previously graduated from the 8th grade in Fossil Creek.

When Bill was fifteen he and his 15 year old childhood sweetheart Goldie ran away to Flagstaff and got married. They must have looked eighteen because they came back with a marriage certificate.

Their marriage was short lived as Goldie's parents didn't approve of their daughter being married so young. Bill's first child was named Floy Mae Helm. When Goldie remarried, she and her new husband raised Floy.

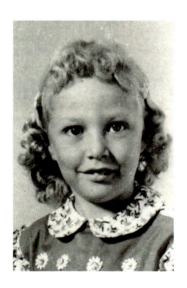

Floy Mae Helm – School Picture – 1954-55

Floy Mae Helm – Picture taken 1949

Bill joins the Navy at Age 17

Bill joined the Navy in 1946 serving his country during World War II. He remembers swabbing the deck aboard the Aircraft Carrier USS Roosevelt.

They sailed to Pearl Harbor to help with the clean up after the Japanese attack there. When Bill was honorably discharged he immediately went back to the Randall Ranch in Bloody Basin.

Soon after this, Bill was a passenger in a car going back to Childs from Camp Verde when it rolled over near the Clear Creek Bridge. The other friends and two hitch hikers (they had picked up along the way) in the vehicle were taken to the hospital in Cottonwood.

The officers assumed Bill was dead, covered him with a blanket and left him. Someone later came out to take the body into town and discovered he was alive.

He was taken to the hospital and then there was a further mix-up. He was put in jail as a drunk even though he had not been drinking. The next day his father arrived and succeeded in getting Bill medical attention. Bill had suffered a skull fracture.

Bill's Family Grows

Bill's second wife was Barbara Lafferty. Children from that marriage are Charles William (Billy) Jr., Randy Lee, and Judith Ann Helm. They lived at the Hot Springs Rock Ranch House until Billy was old enough to go to school. At that time, their mother moved with the children into Cottonwood.

Billy and Randy – Bill's two sons

Randy, Judy and Billy Helm – 1957

Randy Lee Helm and dog Poochie at Rock Ranch House in Childs. Poochie kept Randy from going near the River.

Randy on Allen Parsons at Hot Springs Rock Ranch House

Bill's sons Billy and Randy (above) during school days

Bill would take Billy across the river on Allen Parsons

Chapter 2
Bill's Cowboy Life

When Bill was 13, he became friends with Jake Randall whose parents owned the Hot Springs Ranch at Childs. Bill started working off and on for the Randall family for board and room. Then he started his cowboy career working on the Randall Ranch in Bloody Basin about 30 miles west of Payson, Arizona. This was when his love for the cowboy life, the forests, and outdoors began.

Bill ropin' at Round-up Time

The former owner of the ranch before the Randalls was Pete LaTourette. He went bankrupt, and eventually rounded up all the cattle he could find and took them to Mexico. Earl Heath out of Pine was hired by the Arizona Bank in Prescott to round up the wild cattle and sell them for whatever he could get out of them.

The money would be used to pay off the loan Pete owed the bank. The remaining cattle went wild and these were the cattle Bill and the other cowboys were to find and brand for the Randall Ranch. The Walter (WJ) Randall Family had a 99 year lease on the Bloody Basin cattle range from the 1940's into the 70's.

The Randall family consisted of Walter Randall (WJ) and sons George, Glen, Mill, and son-in-law Lonnie Howard. They obtained a permit from the Forest Service for cattle around 1942. The land then had to be fenced for cattle as there were no fences previously. This range was formerly sheep range. When the fences were built they were used as a division point between the sheep and cattle.

Glen and George Randall

The roundup was held twice a year, spring and fall. Roundup lasted six weeks, and during that time it went from daybreak to dark every day, no days off. The calves were dehorned, earmarked, vaccinated, and branded. The males were castrated before they were old enough to leave their mothers' sides.

The long 60-mile cattle drive started in Bloody Basin in the spring. The steers, bulls, and older cows were shipped out of Pine and the younger cows and calves were left at Long Valley on top of the Mogollon Rim to be shipped in the fall.

Roundup riders had to know the Bloody Basin terrain as well you know your own street. It was taken for granted that they were superb riders and that also they knew how to shoe a horse.

The cowboy provided his own saddle and pad, bridle, lariat, chaps and bedroll. He slept on the ground. He was not choosy about rations. He'd eat beef and biscuits twice a day and make out on a can of juice for lunch. He didn't shave, or worry about baths or changes of underwear, or the sanitary details of his drinking water.

Because of the thick brushy cedar, mesquite, and Manzanita vegetation, cowboys took cow dogs along. A good cow dog was worth two extra cowboys in country like this. Dogs could go into thick brush where cowboys couldn't go.

The roundup was hard work, but a cowboy had a funny feeling that he was lucky to be there. If he didn't feel that way, he quit. (Schubert, 1958)

Many a cowboy walked off the job in Bloody Basin. Bill left a good job in Alaska and came back to Arizona for the Randalls' 1957 spring roundup.

Pay was a dollar per day, with room and board under the stars. Meals consisted of beans, bacon, eggs, biscuits, gravy, and sometimes a rabbit or a deer steak.

Bill always carried a branding/running iron, vaccine gun, and a dehorning saw on his saddle. There were no fences or corrals at that time so the above tasks were done by roping the cattle and tying them down on the open range.

Open range branding and dehorning
Bill's Memories

There were several brands used at that time. Some of the brands were bought from other ranches.

Brands

Grandpa Walt (WJ) Randall's	X Cross
George Randall's	Muleshoe X
Lonnie Howard's	FK Bar
Mill Randall's	S (S ex)
Other brands used by the Randall Brothers and Bill	½, ED, G2

Note: Calves had to be branded the same brand as the mother cow.

Bill dehorning large bull

Usually there were about three or four cowboys to help hold down the cattle, but sometimes I had to perform these tasks by myself. I had four good cow dogs that helped me round up the cattle. I felt the dogs did a better job than some of the cowboys especially in the brush. A cowboy might ride right past cattle hiding in the brush but the cow dogs would smell them and bring the cattle out in the open.

If the cattle starting running away, the dogs would trail them down and stop them. Then I could bring the cattle down to where I could work them. Working them meant doctoring, branding, castrating bulls, etc.

When you have good cow dogs and good cow horses it made the cowboy's job a lot easier. I would always drive the cattle down to lower country with the help of my dogs. I would then leave them standing and looking at me for a while. That would gentle them down.

Bill and his Lasso

Bill Ropes a Deer

I was waiting on George Randall and some other cowboys down at Fossil Mesa and I had my leg over the saddle sittin' there waiting for them to bring the cattle down through this big flat you know how it is lookin' off towards Fossil Creek. I was sittin' there and they was goin' to bring the cattle down through the gate and these two yearlings went outside the fence.

So I went through the gate to bring the yearlings around and we'd hold them up till we brought the herd up and we'd put the yearlings up with the herd. I was sittin' there waitin' and all at once this big ole buck jumped up in front of the herd. He came a boppin' down through there.

There was a low place in the fence right where I was sittin' holdin' these yearlings. That sucker headed right for that low place in the fence and I was about 25 foot from it. I just sat there real still and had my rope over the saddle horn in case the yearlings broke out. I threw that rope on one antler, and my dogs started after him, and the doggone buck was jumpin' around there after my dogs and all at once he seen that doggone ole horse and he come up through there but I kept out of the way and got him on the lower side.

George Randall seen me and came around through the gate and came down there and threw his rope over the butt and the deer just went backwards into his rope and George pulled up on his heels and pulled him down.

Here came ole Chilly Beach with his doggone pickup. Boy, George said, "Don't kill him, don't kill him, we want to just turn him loose." So we turned that ole big buck loose and those two yearlings were there and he went right on up in the herd with the yearlings. We drove them almost to the Hot Springs and by golly that sucker lay down behind some bushes and George said, "Let's leave him." So we left him there and I came back about a week later and he was dead. I guess it must have broke somethin' inside of him or broke his spirit. We drove him about three miles up the Verde toward the Hot Springs.

"Survivin'"

Down here there were a lot of screw worms that year and this little ole calf had a bunch of them in his navel you know. It hadn't healed up good and them ole flies had blowed it. So I went and I caught the little calf. I was ridin' an ole horse called Roanie and that sucker was the most club footed ole horse you ever seen.

Anyway, I caught the calf as the dogs held it up. I doctored the calf and turned that calf up and it followed my horse and wouldn't go back to the cows. Well, I was goin' to jog my horse up through there and cross this gully and out run this calf as he was just a little ole devil. I was goin' to put my dogs on the cow and come back.

So I jogged my horse up and we started across this gully and the horse lost its back feet and came right over on top of me. I was hemmed in this little ole gully, right in the bottom, and the horse was on top of my leg.

It never hurt me because the saddle sort of left me in a little V down there and boy was I working tryin' to get my leg out from under that saddle and I couldn't do it so I reached down and unsnapped my chaps and pulled my boot off. I had no sooner got clear of that horse when that horse went to jumpin' back and forth with all four feet up in the air and tore my saddle all to pieces. If I'd been underneath that sucker I tell you that would have ground me up like hamburger. I was so thankful that horse stayed just as still till I got out from underneath him. I got to thinkin' and I was sure prayin' to the good Lord up above.

Another time, I was up on Verde Saddle, I was by myself, and like a fool I roped this great big sharp horned steer. I would wrap him around a tree like this when we rope 'em and then we'd doggone take a saw and saw his horns off, just make a V round the tree so we got a dally around the tree.

So I was there sawing his horns off and I felt a little slack in my rope. I turned around and I yelled at the ole' horse I was ridin' named Shorty. I threw some rocks at ole Shorty and yelled, "Back up Shorty." Ole Shorty was backin' up and I looked and the doggone rope had broken right there on his horn.

Doggone, there I was with a saw in my hand and that ole steer started draggin' me and he was blowin' snot all over my belly. I had the one horn sawed and the sucker left scrape marks all over my belly and blood all over from where that horn was bleeding. By golly I tell you I was just lucky it wasn't a sharper horn. I tell you that's what I say survivin' out here by yourself you get to thinkin' about it.

Stag and Me

I rode another ole horse called Buttons. I was up above the Hot Springs Hotel and goin' down that fence with the cactus all in it and I was fixin' the fence and ole Buttons had the ringworm real bad and could hardly walk but he liked to doggone get out and go so I took him. I was comin' down the fence and there was this big ole stag. He was next to this here fence and right where the pasture joins in I whipped around there and I opened that gate. I come back and started that stag down the fence and the ole stag broke back and I said well ole Buttons will show him and I roped that big stag.

The stag pulled the horse over and I went off in the cactus. Like ole Jackie, I pulled down my chaps and britches and started pickin' cactus needles out of my butt you know. All at once I heard a commotion and here comes Buttons down to me and the stag was tied to the rope on my saddle horn.

There I was, I tried to run and I fell over on all four, and that ole stag was catchin' me in the butt and he flipped me up in the air. He was blowin' snot all over my butt and doggone I was yellin' at ole Buttons and I got to thinkin' boy that would have made a good video. That ole steer weighed about 1200 pounds. That sucker, by golly, was really workin' me over.

Rattlesnake Bite

Where the East Verde runs into the Verde River there was another cabin about two miles up. The cowboys didn't like staying there because there were so many rattlesnakes and pack rats. There were holes in the floor where they could crawl into the cabin.

It wasn't so bad in the wintertime after the snakes went into hibernation. I was building fence there one time, reached down to pick up a fence post, and was bitten by a rattlesnake. It was too far to ride out horseback so I chose to stay near the East Verde River and soak my hand in the cool water. As a result of the venom from the bite my finger and arm became swollen and very painful.

Jake, a fellow cowboy, lanced my finger, and I sucked on it to get the poison out. Jake then rode to the Hot Springs to get me some snake medicine. About 6 hours later as the sun was goin' down, I heard a horse coming back and the rider was singing and very happy.

Jake brought me a bottle of whiskey that was close to being empty. After about three days, I rode out to the Hot Springs Ranch and soaked my finger in the Hot Springs. I claimed the snake just crawled off and died after biting me but the truth was it died after I shot it.

Memories of Fossil Creek and ranching in Bloody Basin

One time in the bottom of Red Creek Canyon, my horse reared up, came over backwards onto me and broke my leg. The horse had been, unknown to me, eating loco weed. I stayed at Red Creek Canyon cabin for one day.

When my leg became extremely swollen, George Randall, the boss, told me to ride out and get to the hospital which was a distance of about 18 miles. Then the boss asked me to lead out two pack horses. They would be carrying beef to the Hot Springs Ranch which was on my way.

The Randalls built a 20x18 cabin at Red Creek. It was used as a line shack when they were building the fences for cattle. Up Red Creek wash there was a spring that was used to pipe water down to Red Creek Cabin into the water troughs for the cattle. After each flood usually the pipe line had to be repaired. Sometimes the cowboys had to dig down about 4 foot to find the pipe after all the debris had flowed down the wash.

There were five pastures that were used to hold cattle: Houston Basin, Long Mesa, Red Creek, Fossil Creek Mesa, and Eagle Nest. In the spring and fall, the wire and fence posts had to be repaired or replaced.

Hot Springs Ranch house in early days

When Bill was about 13, the Randall Brothers were in the process of building the Hot Springs Ranch house up the river from the Hot Springs Hotel. In the day time he would go up to the ranch house site and gather and haul rocks for the house using an old horse and wagon to haul them.

Aerial view of Hot Springs Ranch

Chaparrals Tuffy Peach and Hank Peach were the people that hauled the salt from Camp Verde to the Hot Springs Ranch site. At that time the salt was used for sheep and Ben Coppel was the person that distributed the salt to the sheep camps. These men also brought salt, food and supplies into the sheep camps. They held a permit for grazing sheep only. (Campbell Francis Company owned the sheep.)

Aerial view of Hot Springs Ranch

Aerial view of Hot Springs Ranch taken in 1970

Bill standing next to "Hot Springs Ranch House" at Childs in 2008

Hot Springs Hotel built and operated by a group of businessmen from Prescott

Don Breckenridge and his family from Michigan would come to work at the Hot Springs Hotel during summers in the early days.

Don tells the story of meeting Bill when he was herding cattle up the banks of the Verde River near the hotel. They became friends and in later years went to Horse Camp together with their metal detectors hoping to find the mother lode. Bill's gold stories are included in this book in another chapter.

Don's daughter Lynn McKay and her husband Phil came back out west and bought property in Camp Verde, Arizona in more recent years. Part of the reason for this was that she had such fond memories of her summers in the Fossil Creek area and the Hot Springs Hotel (see following map).

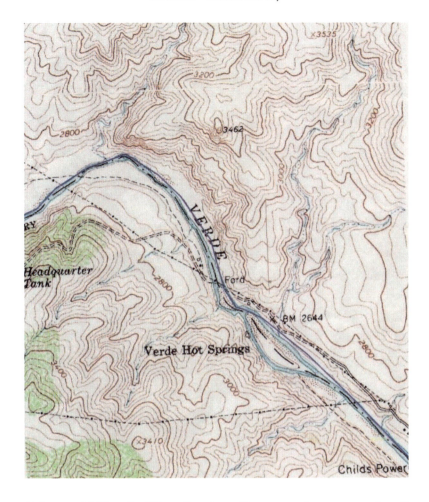

Map of "Verde Hot Springs" area where much of Bill's cowboy life took place

The "Verde Hot Springs" is located a short distance down the Verde River from where the Hot Springs Hotel was. It contains minerals that purportedly sooth pain from arthritis and other physical ailments.

A person has to go to the Childs Campground and hike about 2 miles to reach the Hot Springs. There is high visitation to the Hot Springs year round. The USDA Forest Service has jurisdiction over this whole area at the present time since the Arizona Public Service 100-year lease expired and was not renewed.

The agency tries to control the nudity at the Hot Springs but it is an impossible responsibility.

Cherokee Indian Ben Coppel
Hot Springs Hotel Caretaker
Guide for Zane Grey
Buried In Cornville, AZ

Stories of Ben Coppel
By Bill Helm

The first time I was in Bloody Basin I went there with a Cherokee Indian named Ben Coppel to deliver the salt to the sheep camps. We were packing salt out from the old salt house where now the ranch house sits above the old Hot Springs. The salt came from the salt mine at Camp Verde, Arizona. It was packed in down the river and put in the salt house.

They had about 12 or 14 pack horses and they'd come down and unload them and go back to Camp Verde and get another load. That is how they got the salt in for the cattle in those days.

We had to pack salt clear through Bloody Basin and into Red Creek, LX Bars, and down to Horse Camp and Long Mesa. So we had around 6 pack horses and 2 were loaded with our personal belongings, camp stuff, and grain.

We'd go into Horse Camp and make that our permanent camp and then we'd go along the ridges at Long Mesa, Red Creek, Yellow Jack, and Monroe Canyon and leave salt for the cattle. And I was just a kid about twelve or thirteen years old and Ben was always afraid I was going to get lost.

We came in there to an old mine above Horse Camp and it had an old iron door on it. I was beating on this old padlock on this iron door trying to get it off and Old Ben came out there and jumped all over me and said: "You don't try to break into another man's property. That's been locked for years and the owner will probably be back."

I learned a lesson about respecting another man's property that day and that was the end of me trying to break into the old mine shaft.

After we got back to Horse Camp, we'd go back to the Hot Springs and then we'd take salt out in different directions from there. There was only a little 6 x 6 tin shed at Horse Camp to store the salt in at that time.

Zane Grey, dentist and author, came to Arizona in the years 1918, 1919, 1920, as a hunter and sportsman and hired Ben Coppel as his guide. From there, he was successful in hunting deer, bear, elk, and mountain lion in the Bloody Basin and Pine areas.

Grey used this very country and experiences he had in the real West as material for his two novels "Under the Tonto Rim" and "To The Last Man."

Grey gave Ben a hunting rifle as a gift. Ben always treasured it. (Schubert, 1958)

"My Friend Ben"
By Clint Self

I knew an old cowboy a long time ago
Here in the old Verde Valley
He had fingers missing from both hands
He had trouble learning to dally.

His legs were bowed like harness hames
From years of riding a horse
He didn't say much but meant what he said
And his manner of speech was course

He drove around in his Model A Ford
That never did have good brakes,
And he much preferred a bowl of beans
To the daintiest kind of cakes.

His heart was big and his word was good
And he always seemed content,
And I noticed from the times I spent with him
He was welcome wherever he went.

He didn't have a lot of wealth
And didn't seem to care,
But whatever money he happened to have
He was always willing to share.

The years went by and Ben grew old
And then he passed away,
We buried my friend on the top of a hill
And that's where he is today.

Man of War, Bill, and Ben Coppel

The Randalls had just bought the cattle ranch from Earl Heath and this was in 1940.

I remember when they were building the old ranch house. I used to come down every chance I got to the old hotel and stay with a Cherokee Indian named Ben Coppel. He was the caretaker for the Hot Springs Hotel at the time. A horse had fallen on Ben and broke some of his ribs so I went down and loaded all the pack horses. Ben had a few head of cattle running around on the range there and that's where we were taking salt out to.

In 1941 or 1942, I had been working for Franklin Godard. He had a little horse for his daughter Patsy and Shelly Richards had tried to break it. It was just too much of a little old horse for Patsy and Franklin was going to send it down for dog chow at the packing company in Phoenix.

I talked Franklin out of this horse when I was helping with the roundup. Franklin called him "Man of War." He said when he goes to bucking he is just a regular little man at war. I was trying to buy the horse or work him out as I was being paid nearly nothing.

He paid me $10 for helping move the cattle off the mountain and then we'd go from Fossil Creek to Long Valley and then I'd come back home to Fossil Creek. The horse had a Diamond U brand on him which was Franklin's brand. So Franklin told my mother I wanted the horse and asked her if she would let me have him. My mother said she would let me have him.

Franklin said, "I won't sell the horse to him but I'll give the horse to him because if Bill gets hurt I'd feel real bad about it." So I took the horse up to Fossil Creek. I was little afraid of him because they told me how hard he bucked so I fed him hay and kept him in the little corral there. The little old horse would follow me around and I'd grain him and talk to him. I took him across the crick and got on old Fossil Creek road and slipped on him and I sit there. That little horse looked around and smelled both my legs and I sit there and he wouldn't even move, boy he was just all blowed up.

I said, "Well, I'll sit here just as long as you will till you take a step." So the old horse finally took a step, and I reached down and patted him a little bit, he took another step, I patted him a little bit and scratched him on the neck, took another step and we just went right off and that little horse never did buck with me. That little horse would follow me all around from then on.

I went down to help old Ben Coppel and I took this horse and the little black horse I had named Blacky. This black horse was a Welsh and Shetland; he was awful small. I was outgrowing him anyway but I took him along with me. He was an ornery little horse to catch. I could catch Man of War anyplace. I would whistle and Man of War would come runnin'.

So this time when Ben had these broken ribs I went down with him and I took the Diamond U horse. We got down to the hotel and packed salt and all the goodies onto the horses and I took this little black horse and my personal belongings and we went into Horse Camp.

It was the first time we stayed at Horse Camp. There was nothing there but an old sycamore tree and old wild cow trap. We put all the horses into this wild cow trap. I took them up there and took their nosebags off (made out of gunny sacks and they went over their ears). We put a can of grain in the bottom of the sack for each horse and then hung the sack over their head.

When each horse finished eating we'd take them off their head and the next morning we went through the same procedure. This time I took the horses up to the cow trap and I never closed the triggers good.

The next morning all the horses were gone. When we got up, old Ben starting jumping on me good when he saw that the horses were gone. He said, "Well, you are just going to have to walk to Red Creek from Horse Camp which was about eight miles. You are going to have to see if you can find them horses and after you find them you are going to have to catch them and bring them back to Horse Camp because I can't walk.

So he was cooking breakfast and he was mad. I said, "This little old Diamond U horse that I call Man of War will be back before we finish breakfast." Ben said, "Hell he will."

So we just finishing up breakfast and I was getting ready to take off and I heard a nicker on top of the hill and there came that horse, he was standing right in the skyline. I yelled at him, and he came a running down that trail and slid up into our camp. I had all the nosebags ready to fill for all the other horses and I hung a nosebag on him and let him eat a little bit, put my saddle on him while he was eating.

Old Ben Coppel said, "Well, if I didn't see it, I wouldn't believe it. I never saw a horse leave other horses and come back looking for somebody." I rode the horse down and got all the other horses and come back to Horse Camp. So from there we packed back up and went back to the Hot Springs. We stayed there at the hotel.

There was an old electric oven, and I remember Ben had left some old pinto beans in there and they had soured and how they stunk as you could smell them. He went to cook them and this was when I first knew of penicillin. He poured me out some in a plate and he took some and he cooked some old biscuits there. He said, "They are good for you, go ahead and eat 'em, they won't hurt you, I eat them all the time, little sour." I couldn't go 'em, I just made me a sandwich out of some honey he had there and ate it. I remember him eating those old sour beans though and he never wasted or threw anything out, I don't care whether things were covered with mold, you better not throw it out.

He'd kill a deer and make jerky for his dogs. He had about 4 or 5 dogs around there. Anyway, I headed out to Irving and I remember old Ben always had an old watermelon patch and a vegetable garden too.

One day I picked the biggest watermelon I could find in his garden. I packed it all the way from the Hot Springs Ranch to Irving and my dad and I put it on ice. When we cut it, it was still green as a gourd and we couldn't eat it. When Ben came by and Dad told him about the watermelon he was sure mad at me for picking it.

When I was 13 or 14 years-old, I remember riding Man of War into Camp Verde to go to a movie - a distance of approximately 30 miles one way. I would leave the gates open and would turn my horse loose when I arrived at the theatre as I planned to catch a ride back to Fossil Creek in my brother's vehicle.

My brother was the operator for TAPCO Power Plant just north of Clarkdale at the time so I would go there for my ride home. My horse would find his way back home at Irving and I would close the gates on my way home within the next day or two.

About Chaps by Bill Helm

Some people think chaps are for looks. In my time, I had several pair. I had to have pockets as I carried my gun and "I" rings for branding, vaccine gun, medicine, a couple of small rag syringes for worm medicine, little rope "strings", staples, horseshoe nails and a horseshoe.

I never went anywhere without my chaps on. I would ride along a barbed wire fence, stiffin' out when the fence was too close and inches from my leg.

I would ride through wait-a-minute bushes and oak brush and all kinds of stuff. My chaps sure helped when I jumped off my horse to tie a calf or work cattle or a colt that wanted to kick me.

If you got a hole in them when going through a fence you just put a patch on them. Sometime you put a patch on top of a patch.

I sure hated to retire a pair of chaps and to have to break in a new pair. You always had to re-do the pockets as new chaps came with pockets just for looks.

I had Ronny Randall pick me up a pair of chaps out of Mexico. He brought back a pair of those good looking chaps and a saddle.

We were riding upon Pine Mountain and had a bunch of wild cattle. I roped a 3-year old steer and tied the rope to my saddle horn. When the steer hit the end of the rope, he took my saddle horn and rope with him. My new chaps were torn all to pieces from riding through the wait-a-minute and oak brush, too. I went back to my old saddle and original chaps.

Lion Hunting

**Bill's friend and lion hunting partner, Zeke
(Bill in Background)**

Zeke Taylor was one of the first cowboys in the Verde Valley. He became a cowboy at the age of 13 when he took his mom's cattle to the Apache Maid Ranch on the Mogollon Rim and worked for Jim Ralston.

His dad had passed away and his mother had to sell the ranch and move from Rimrock to Camp Verde where there was school for Zeke's brothers and sisters. Zeke worked for many ranches on the Rim and in the Verde Valley and also ran his own cattle. Bill met Zeke at a roping event at

Bill Gray's Ranch between Cottonwood and Sedona around 1940. Later on Bill lived at the Riverside Trailer Park that Zeke built and managed.

Zeke also provided the horses and other stock for the companies out of Hollywood that were making films in Sedona in those early years. One of Zeke's horses named Unik was ridden by James Stewart in the movie Broken Arrow. In later years, Zeke gave that horse to Bill.

Zeke also had a lion in a cage that was used for scenes in the movies. One day Bill went with Zeke and Elmer Purtyman to the movie set on Jackass Flats to let the lion out of the cage so the hound dogs could chase it in the scene that was being filmed.

Bill ran trap lines at Stehr Lake and in the Bloody Basin area for many years. He caught all kinds of varmints and sold their pelts. He was getting his hair cut by Milt the Barber in Clarkdale one day. Milt was bragging on the hound dogs he owned and wanted to take them out lion hunting.

Bill told Milt where there might be a lion for his dogs to chase. Bill, Milt, and the hound dogs went out to Stehr Lake where Bill also planned to check his traps.

They found a lion track but the hound dogs were more interested in chasing a deer that was nearby. They ended up just taking the dogs back to Clarkdale empty handed.

Bill wanted to pursue catching the lion that made the track so he and Zeke went back to the area. There was a lion caught in one of the traps by one toe. When Bill got close the lion ripped his toe off and ran over the next hill. Bill shot at it and thought he might have wounded it. Bill and Zeke went after it. They heard it buzzing in a nearby cave.

Bill asked Zeke to hold a flashlight so he could get a shot at it. The lion was up above Bill and Zeke. When Bill shot it he had to jump out of the way as it fell right where he had been standing. They proceeded to pull it out of the cave by the tail and to the truck.

Bill and Zeke then went to a local bar for a drink after their wild adventure. The drunker Zeke got the wilder the story got. Pretty soon Zeke had Bill pulling the lion out of the cave by the tail alive. Zeke reported the kill to the Cattle Association, he and Bill then split the $75 bounty.

Another time, Bill was hunting in the MTs and shot a lion with his 22 pistol. An acquaintance of Bill's named Odie Marksbank was bow hunting for white tail deer in the same area and approached Bill to say hello. When Bill told him he had shot and killed the lion with his 22 pistol Odie didn't believe him until he saw the dead lion.

Bill shot many lions over the years as the ranchers and Cattle Association were glad to pay the $75 bounty and Bill enjoyed the sport and needed the money. Lions enjoy eating young calves and out on the open range the calves are easy prey.

Professional Lion Hunters

Successful lion hunter Bill and daughter Marie

Sally May House – 1949

John and Surrue Gerken came to Fossil Creek in 1945 from Queens, NY. Surrue's son (Frank Owens) was 4 years old when they arrived. They lived at the Sally May house for several years. Surrue's parents Frank and Surrue Ann (Nana) Vanderhoef also lived in the Sally May House.

The house was named after a woman named Sally May who owned and ran the dance hall in the area. The dance hall was also used as a gathering place where meetings and dances were held for the families that lived there. Another Fossil Creek resident Franklin Godard called for the square dances.

The Gerkens came west to Fossil Creek as Surrue had chronic asthma and could no longer survive in New York. At Fossil Creek they raised sheep, cattle, chickens, and also had dogs, horses, and a cow. Surrue milked the cow and had milk and eggs for her own use but also sold them to other families.

Medical supplies had to be stored at the Gerken home as the closest medical facility was about 30 miles away in Cottonwood. At the age of ten, Surrue's son Frank learned how to give his mother injections for her asthma when she would have a severe attack. Many times he drove her into Cottonwood for a stay in the hospital.

When it rained, the Fossil Creek road was very dangerous as it turned to solid mud. There are several canyons along that road that one could slide into very easily when the road is wet and slick. It was also dangerous in the summer when it got very dry and "washboardy". If one traveled too fast it was easy to be bounced right over the edge.

Bill knew this family well as his dad worked with John at the power plant. When Frank was older he would sometimes join Bill to take salt to the cattle via horseback.

Frank Gerken Owens, Bill, and Billy Helm taking salt out to the sheep and cattle at Fossil Creek – 1950's

Frank Vanderhoef, Dixon Lewis, John Gerken, Frank Gerken (Owens) – Frank Vanderhoef, John Gerken, and Frank Gerken lived at the Sally May House

The Art Newberry family also lived in the Sally May house at one time. They had 9 children and the oldest was named John. Bill and John (sometimes called Jackie) have many memories of growing up in Fossil Creek. They also built fences together and had other experiences in Bloody Basin over the years. Below are some of the stories Bill enjoys telling about some of these happenings.

Jackie learns to Drive

One day Jackie came down where I was checking out a herd of heifers in a pasture to see if they had calved yet. I had to check them every other day or so. I was driving an old jeep pickup with an old horse named Dobbin in the back. You didn't even need a horse trailer for him as he would just jump up in the back of the pickup.

I thought Jackie might want to learn to drive. I asked Jackie and he said, "No I can't do that, I don't know enough about it." So I went down to the lower end of this pasture and dumped the horse out. I told Jackie he was going to drive the pickup or he would have to walk back to the ranch. I went off in the bushes and watched him.

He looked, looked, and looked to see where I went and pretty quick he got behind the wheel of the old pickup. It was in low range and went, "errrrr, errrr," up the old sandy wash. There was one place that erosion had washed out and he went off in that hole but with 4-wheel drive he came back up and that was when Jackie learned to drive, right there.

Another time, there was a bunch of javelinas and I took after them horseback and got 'em down in the brush and I said, "Come on down here and let's rope one, Jackie." He was up on top of this ridge. He said a real nasty word and then he said, "Yeah, just go ahead, I'm not gonna' help you." Boy, I tell you he'd chew me out and cuss me out sometimes.

Building fence at Monroe Canyon

We were building a fence down through Monroe Canyon. I was ridin' a couple of colts and breaking 'em and I was ridin' one one day and one the next day. Jackie said, "That ole diamond horse you're breakin' there is gentle. Can I ride him?"

He was always petting and currying him. I said, "Well I don't see why you can't just ride him down the fence, we're not after cattle or nothing". So we get over there and we wire stays in the fence and I was going up dragging stays and he was on one side of the fence and I was on the other.

So we'd left our lunch hanging on the fence way up country there you know where we started out. So I said, "Jackie it's getting close to noon so why don't you ride back up on diamond and get our lunch and all of our stuff and bring it back down. He had a bag full of staples and he put it over his saddle horn and came on down the fence.

Like I said I was on one side of the fence and he was on the other. Pretty soon here came Jackie down the ridge and the wind was blowin' and everything. So he stayed on his horse and put our lunch over on the pole. He had that bag of staples there and when he went to put it over the fence, the wind caught his jacket. It hit that colt in the front shoulder, the colt went straight up, Jackie fell off and his big foot hung in the stirrup.

Down through there that horse went dragging him, through the cactus, and there was nothing I could do 'cause I was on one side of the fence and he was on the other. I couldn't run and catch the horse or nothin'. So the first thing I thought about doin' as the horse was going around in circles dragging him through the cactus and I thought he would be dragged to death so I grabbed my 30-30 rifle and went up the fence.

I knew the horse would head for Horse Camp. So here comes the horse buckin' and kickin' and Jackie wasn't hung to him. His ole big boot came off in the stirrup and I went down there and there was Jackie pickin' cactus out of his butt. I went over and said, "Are you hurt very bad?"

He said, "No." I said, "Let me pick some cactus out of you there, where you can't reach 'em." He picked up a bunch of rocks and yelled, "Get the hell out of here." Then I started laughin' when I could see he wasn't hurt. The ole horse doubled back and came back to my horse. I tell you I would have shot that horse as it would have been the only way to get him loose.

There was another time over here though at the same fence where Jackie got almost drug to death. When we first started the fence we had some help. There was Lonnie, and I and Jackie, and some kid that Lonnie had brought up named Dowel.

So I was checking some cattle back up country and all at once I heard my dogs down there and I thought they got some cows down in the brush. I looked off the ridge and this big ole buck was after them doggone dogs. Great big sucker!

The brush was between me and the buck and the buck would go back in the brush and the dogs would get to yellin' and yappin' at him and then he would run after the dogs. I slipped around real quick. I didn't have a gun with me, and that ole big buck he jumped after the dogs and I threw my rope on him. I caught him by one horn and that sucker went to jumpin' around there. I was ridin' a big ole black horse and he was sort of an ornery horse anyway and that buck came around there and jobbed him in the rump and that horse bucked me off. I had the rope tied to my saddle horn and down through there they went.

Here I was brushing everything off me 'cause I got bucked off. I looked and they got hung up in these doggone weeds down there then the horse went one way and the deer went the other way. So I was yellin' and squallin' for Jackie to come up there and help me and no one would come.

So finally I got around in back of the buck. The ole horse had him pulled up about two foot from a doggone tree and I took me a big ole rock and hit him right between the horns you know and knocked him down on his knees and slit his throat.

Gosh darn we had venison. I said, "Why didn't somebody come up here and help me." Jackie said," I was trying to but ole Lonnie wouldn't let us, he said ole Bill will take care of himself." That sucker had a set of horns on him you wouldn't believe. Anyway he left big ole marks on my horse.

Bill packed up and going to Horse Camp Canyon before the cabin was built and before any roads were built in to it. Bill leading Great Dane dog named Buster.

Chapter 3
Horse Camp

Horse Camp before cabin was built in Horse Camp Canyon. Almy Hunt in checkered shirt and Lonnie Howard in background. Horse was named Burry.

Two other cowboys, Art Hargrave and Lonnie Howard, and I built a line shack cabin in Horse Camp Canyon in the early forties. We dismantled a small cabin at Childs that was used to store salt for sheep and carried it by horseback about 12 miles to Horse Camp Canyon as there were no roads at that time.

Lonnie Howard brought nails and cement from Phoenix as far as he could in an old jeep pickup. These supplies were brought the rest of the way to the Horse Camp Cabin site horseback. It took about a month to build the tin shack cabin that ended up about twice the size of the original cabin. The cowboys then had a place to stay especially during roundup. I carved my name in a small tree in the front yard of the cabin.

Bill Helm's name six feet up in a tree at Horse Camp in Horse Camp Canyon

Horse Camp cabin in Horse Camp Canyon in early years

Art Hargrave on Chief provides the venison

Bill Helm on Buck and Art Hargrave on Shorty
Two of the three original cowboys who built the
Horse Camp Cabin

Bill was staying at Horse Camp Cabin during a recent deer hunt. He headed toward Red Creek Ranch during the evening in hopes of seeing a deer to shoot. On the way he met a fellow driving toward Horse Camp Canyon also hunting.

They stopped to chat in the usual way when one is out hunting. Hunter conversations usually include asking, how's it going? Have you seen any deer sign? How long have you been out hunting? Are you camped near here?

The fellow Bill met was camping near Red Creek and when Bill told him he was staying at Horse Camp Cabin the man said, "I helped built that cabin." Bill said, "Really, I helped build that cabin, who in the hell are you?" The fellow said "I'm Art Hargrave, Who in the hell are you?"

They hadn't seen each other for more than fifty years and didn't recognize each other. Art and his wife came to the Helm residence in Camp Verde shortly after that and both families had a great time visiting about the old and present days and exchanging pictures.

Bill and Art reunited at Horse Camp Cabin

Bill, Grandson Matt, and Billie

Bill and Bo at Horse Camp

Present barn - bunkhouse at Horse Camp

Bill (in back) Toni, Matt, Blue, Billy, Bo

Bill and author Kevin Leonard at Horse Camp – 2007

Kevin Leonard has explored the Bloody Basin country over the last few years. He has interviewed Bill about what he has come across as Bill knows that country like the back of his hand.

Kevin has written two books about his experiences as he has been out in the wild for several weeks at a time with his horse and pack horse. The books are called, "Ride with Me," and "Some Trust in Horses." There are four pages about Bill in Kevin's most recent book.

Smoke, Toni, Bill, and Bo at Horse Camp

Bill, Bo, Toyota pickup and bunkhouse at Horse Camp

Barn and bunkhouse at Horse Camp in earlier days

Bill, Billie, Cody and Gus at Horse Camp - 2012

Bill, Cody, Charlsa, and Gus Phillips - 2012

Bill in horse trailer shade at Horse Camp

Sign Bill put outside the Horse Camp cabin door to discourage vandalism

Smoke listening to Billie sing at Horse Camp

Bill and his mule Cracker looking into Horse Camp Cabin

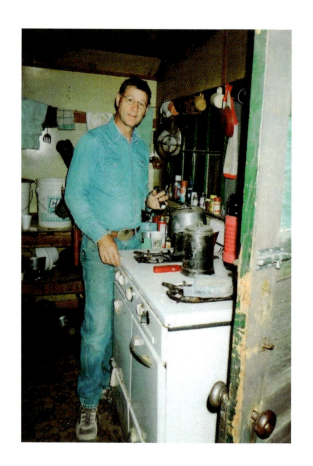

Bill's son Randy cooking at
Horse Camp Cabin

Kitchen and cabinet area in Horse Camp Cabin

Barrel wood stove in Horse Camp Cabin

Horse Camp after snow storm

Billie making snow people at Horse Camp

Billie and her father Bill Crose at Horse Camp

Cracker, Ben, Billie and Bill going hunting

Bill, Smoke, Ben, Cracker, Billie, Midnight

Successful deer hunt (below)

Grandpa Bill and his grandson Mikey

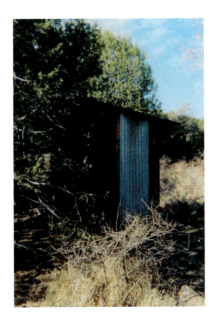

Outhouse at Horse Camp – tree is the only door

Return trip from Houston Creek in Bloody Basin

Bill's old 1981 4-wheel drive yellow Toyota pickup pulled Randy's Dodge truck with three people inside and a horse trailer with three horses inside up steep Childs hill as a result of the fuel pump going out on Randy's truck. Billie, with her son Ben, drove the Nissan pickup and their horse trailer up the hill behind Bill and Randy.

At the top, Bill took over the Nissan and the horse trailer. Billie, following behind, drove the 1981 Toyota on up Fossil Creek Road. About two miles before Billie and Ben reached the Highway 260, all of a sudden, their lights went out and the Toyota quit. Billie managed to drive to the edge of the road and into a small ditch.

It was a long time before Bill came back looking for them. The battery couldn't be jumped because it had blown up. Billie and Ben were stuck in the Toyota in the dark while Bill went back to get a different battery. Ben was pretty young then and had his mom lock the doors and roll up the windows as he was afraid a coyote or lion was going to get them. When Bill came back, they managed to get the rest of the way home.

Bill and Billie's problem-filled road experiences on the Bloody Basin Road

Some of Bill and Billie's Bloody Basin arduous road experiences over the years in their 1981 Toyota 4WD pickup and their old 4-wheel drive Dodge pickup.

1. The road was so bad that the drive line fell out. Bill crawled under the pickup and was able to take the bolts out of the 4WD drive spots and put them into the two wheel

drive spots where the bolts had broken off. Billie thought they were going to be stuck for several days.

2. Another time when the drive line fell out Billie was able to crawl under the pickup with Bill to put new bolts in. The bolts had completely broken off and were missing.

3. One night the battery case broke and the lights went out. Bill was able to bungee the case back together to get the lights back on. They could finally see the road again and find their way back to horse camp cabin.

4. In this instance, they were going up a steep hill between Long Mesa and Horse Camp and ran out of gas. The switch wouldn't work to engage the second gas tank. Bill crawled under the pickup and was able to wire round that switch in order to access the second tank. They then went on their way. While they were stopped a jeep was able to squeeze around and it didn't even stop to see if they needed any help.

5. When Bill and Billie were on their way home from Horse Camp, it was raining and the road was very slick. They were pulling a horse trailer with two horses in it. The road was "extra slanting" coming down and the truck and trailer slid into the ditch. Bill had Billie take the horse out of the horse trailer on the ditch side of the pickup and hold him in the road. Bill then drove up the ditch, pulling the horse trailer, as he had seen a culvert a ways up. He then drove over the culvert to get back on the road. For a moment, Billie didn't realize what he was doing and thought he was leaving her behind. She was able to slide up the muddy road leading that horse and put him back in

the trailer. Once again, they were on their way. They were all wet and muddy but didn't care a bit.

6. They always carried extra bolts, bailing wire, electric wire, flash lights, batteries, gas, water, food, and tools with them on those trips just to be safe. It was before cell phones were available.

Gila Monster in the Road

Bill and Billie were coming out of Bloody Basin when they spotted this Gila monster in the middle of the road. Billie wanted to take a picture of it so Bill got out of the pickup to try to keep it in the road so she could get a good shot.

The Gila monster headed for the brush and when Bill tried to head him off he tripped on a rock and almost fell on it. That happening was a little more excitement than they wanted, but they did get this picture.

Bill and Billie like going to the Horse Camp Cabin in Bloody Basin. They have hunted quail, javelina, and deer there in past years. They hunt horseback and have also participated in some of the more recent roundups on the Red Creek Ranch.

Bill and Billie have written and recorded a song called "Round Up in Bloody Basin" that tells about what is out there and how it was when Bill was a cowboy there when he was a young man. (Contact the author with respect to ordering copies of a CD that contains several original songs including "Round-up in Bloody Basin". Phone 928-567-3108.)

Memories of Visit to Horse Camp and Sheep Bridge
Written by Billie Helm

April 18 – 23, 2004

We arrived late afternoon the first day. Road in was good until after Yellow Jack Tank. We saw several coveys of quail on the way in.

Present were Billy, Toni, Matt, Krysti, Bill and I (Billie) all members of the Helm family.

Helms First morning – Rock Wren came through hole in the door to its nest up in the corner of the ceiling next to the door. There were four eggs in the nest. The Wrens would not come into Horse Camp when the ringtail cats were here. It has been a couple of years since Rock Wrens were here.

We could also hear other birds as the sun came up including dove in the distance. I don't know what happened to all the ringtails.

Second day – we went to Sheep Bridge fishing. Toni drove us there. Some of us rode in the back of the pickup. We stopped at Red Creek to dig up worms for bait. It was eleven miles from the turn off to Sheep Bridge and it seemed like at least 30 because of the bad, rocky road.

Bill Helm, Grandson Matt Helm, Billy Helm, and Granddaughter Krysti Jenkins

We saw two turkey vultures fly off a cactus on the way in. Toni and I also saw two roadrunners, one had a lizard in his mouth.

We took pictures of the new bridge and what remains of the old Sheep Bridge. We only fished at the river crossing – and we had no bites.

Bill and Billie at new Sheep Bridge

Matt and Krysti sat in the water, splashed, and had fun. Bo and Buddy (our dogs) also had fun in the water. Bill slept on a sleeping bag in the shade as the ride in gave him a shoulder and headache.

Billy, Toni and I cast our lines in with no luck. I lost two sinkers, hooks, and bait to being hung up in rocks. Billy waded across the river to get his hook unstuck. He took his shoes off which killed his feet but he didn't fall in.

Krysti slept with her head in my lap almost all the way back to Horse Camp. Matt was cranky and tired so he went to bed early. Bill and I went to bed right after dinner too.

Third morning, Bill and I got up early. We drank our tea outside by the campfire. Bill had his radio on real low and we listened to KRIM radio station out of Payson.

They told about the first KFC restaurant ever being torn down in Murray, Utah. They will build a museum in its place to commemorate the event. Originally Colonel Sanders just called it Fried Chicken. Someone told him how good chicken from Kentucky was so he renamed his restaurant Kentucky Fried Chicken.

I went for a walk up the road towards Long Mesa. Bo went with me. Our son Randy buzzed the cabin in his Air Coop.

Chapter 4
Hydroelectric Power Plants

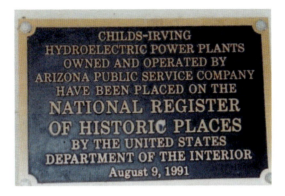

While hydroelectric power enabled growth and development within the central Arizona mining industry, it also helped to spur the growth of Phoenix and the Salt River Valley. The Arizona Power Company and the Childs-hydroelectric plant also had an impact on the development of Jerome, Prescott, Mayer, and other central Arizona communities.

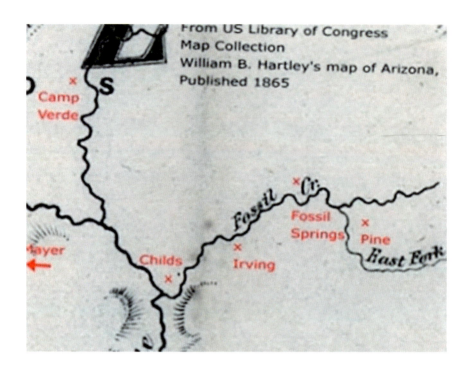

US Library of Congress Map of Fossil Creek Area

Fossil Creek on a normal day

Fossil Creek flooded - 1949

In the early 1900's, a Yavapai County cattleman named Lew Turner told his partner at the old Army Post in Camp Verde that the biggest spring he ever heard of gushed forth under the rocks one hundred yards or so below where the Apache Trail crossed the biggest canyon on the way to Strawberry over in Gila County. He told him the water from these springs covered stocks and stone, ferns and rocks with a formation which made them look like fossil.

They named the creek Fossil Creek. Later Lew Turner filed for the water rights at the springs and appropriated the use of the water for himself. The original rights were made by notice posted February 26, 1900.

A subsequent amended appropriation was made on May 6, 1901. He succeeded in interesting capital in 1902.

An engineering study was made for the best way to utilize the water from these springs to develop power.

It was found that a large market existed for this power in the mines and towns of Yavapai County. Turner, along with F. E. Jordon, Edwin Meek, and Iva Tutt organized the Arizona Power Company (APCO) and planned two power plants that same year. Some construction and development work was done then but attempts to finance the project were unsuccessful.

The Electric Operating Construction Company organized by Messra Masson, Veile and others started construction upon completion of financing and execution of contracts for power sales to the United Verde Copper Company in 1907.

The Arizona Power Company (a Maine corporation) was organized in 1908 and took over the assets of the Electric Operating Construction Company and Arizona Power Company.

On March 28, 1908, changes to the APCO articles of incorporation were enacted. APCO became TAPCO (The Arizona Power Company) and in April 1908, the reorganized company began construction of the Childs plant.

Power demand continued to increase and by the end of 1914, because of World War I, the high price of copper and revival of the mining industry, TAPCO was encouraged to build a second hydroelectric plant on Fossil Creek in 1915.

Mule teams were used for transporting most of the supplies to the construction site

Mule teams transported all of the material to the plant site over a road that was built from the nearest railroad at Mayer, Arizona. The road went across Tule Mesa, and over the Verde River rim to Childs. The largest piece of apparatus needed was the generator stator that required a 26-mule team. Probably the most important man in the construction of the Childs Plant was the muleskinner.

This portion of the plan consisted of the installation of the power plant at Childs and a double circuit 44,000 volt transmission line from Childs to Prescott by way of Mayer and Poland Junction. It also consisted of a double circuit tap extending from Poland Junction to the mines in Jerome.

Due to the almost superhuman efforts on the part of the construction crews this project was completed, and Generator No. 1 was put on the line carrying load to the mines in Jerome on June 18, 1909. Generator No. 2 was placed in service on July 22, 1909 and Generator No. 3 was placed in service the latter part of the same year.

The water flume for the new plant was constructed using cement and wire mesh. Nearly 8800 feet of concrete flume was constructed. The flume was originally uncovered and crews of Indian workers were employed to keep the flume free of algae growth. A cover was built over the flume at a later date to prevent algae growth.

To ensure an adequate, continuous supply of water to the Childs plant, Stehr Lake was built in an old dry lake bed and it covered 27.5 acres. The lake bed made the system possible by providing a reservoir to run the Childs plant when repairs and maintenance activities shut off the flume's water flow. The reservoir was created by constructing two earth filled dams at either end of the lake bed. (Arizona Public Service, 1992)

When construction of the flume began up a steep hill from Stehr Lake some of the Indian workers quit as they thought it "was evil spirits that made water run uphill."

Indian Camp – Construction workers working on flume for power plant lived here

All of the men employed were Apache and Mojave Indians excepting the foremen, sub-foreman, and timekeeper. Construction workers earned about $2 per day. The labor force consisted of "600 men and 400 mules hauling more than 150 wagons..." (Masson 1910). Workers lived in construction camps composed of wikyups, tents, and wooden structures.

Building surveyors stayed in during construction phase (picture taken in 2003)

Irving Power Plant under Construction

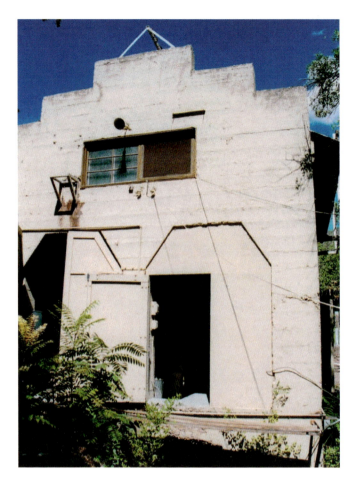

South side of Irving Power Plant

With still more requests for power than what could be provided, TAPCO announced the need for a third plant.

This increasing need for power to the mining industry and to the United Verde Clarkdale smelter led to the construction of the TAPCO steam generating plant in Clarkdale. On September 1, 1917, this steam plant began operating and doubled the amount of electricity available.

Agreements between United Verde Copper Company and the Arizona Power Company provided this additional power and the Companies completed the TAPCO Plant, the Irving Plant and a transmission line connecting the Irving and Childs Plants.

Bill's brother George was an operator at the TAPCO Plant in Clarkdale for many years. He then transferred to Fossil Springs where he was the gate keeper that monitored the flow of water at Irving. Later on he became the Chief Operator at the Childs power plant.

In 1927 a transmission line was constructed between Prescott and Constellation to provide electricity to mines in the Wickenburg area. Additional power was routed to Prescott for local use via a new line from Mingus Mountain through Lonesome Valley. TAPCO purchased the Ash Fork and Seligman electric systems in 1929-1930, and built new transmission lines from Prescott to Ashfork and Seligman.

By 1932, electricity was also being sold to the Town of Wickenburg and to the Flagstaff Electric Light Company. The hydroelectric power from Fossil Creek was created for the mines of Yavapai County. (Arizona Public Service, 1992)

FOSSIL SPRINGS WILDERNESS

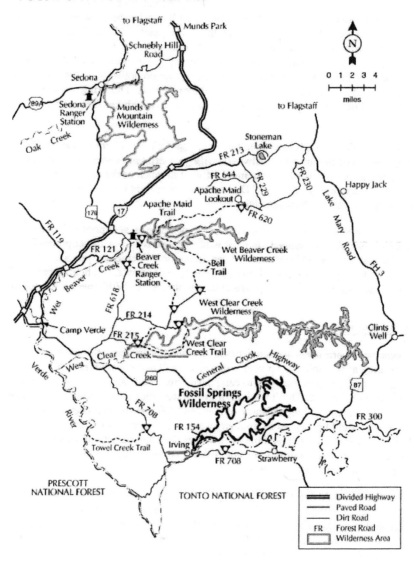

Fossil Springs Wilderness Map

George Helm (Bill's Father) operated the Irving Power Plant for several years

Irving Power Plant governor, water wheel, and generator – monitored by operator George Helm

The Irving Power Plant was started in 1915 and completed in April 1916. My father, George Henry Helm, started work at the Childs/Irving Power Plants in 1916.

George Henry Helm (Bill's Father) at Irving Power Plant using crate to transport mail and other items across Fossil Creek

George Helm calling home

Typical company owned employee house at Irving Power Plant (2003 picture)

"Childs-Irving Hydroelectric Facilities" consisted of two 20th-century power plants, a dam, and related infrastructure along or near Fossil Creek in the U.S. state of Arizona. The complex was named an Historic Mechanical Engineering Landmark in 1971 and was added to the National Register of Historic Places 20 years later. Decommissioned in 2005, the plants no longer produce electricity, and much of the infrastructure—including the dam, the Irving Power Plant, and thousands of feet of concrete flumes—have been removed, and the creek's original flow has been restored." The preceding paragraph and information contained therein is **Quoted from Wikipedia and Wikimedia.**

Childs Plant # 1 Tailrace*

NOTE: *Definition of Tailrace: a race (trench) for conveying water away from a point of industrial application (as a waterwheel or turbine) after use.*

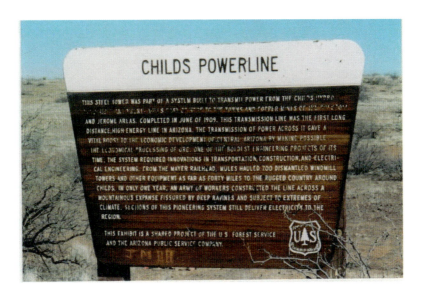

Forest service sign – landmark for Childs Powerline

Looking down at Childs Power Plant from top of a hill

Sharp curve going into Childs – location of Childs Power Plant

Jack Francis walked the flume every day checking for leaks – 1935 license plate on car

Jack Francis' mom leading Jack Francis' dad who was blind
Note: Flume in backgound

Lewis brothers: Richard, Dixon, Floyd, and Gene Hubbs (without hat)
All went to school at the one room schoolhouse mentioned earlier

Chapter 5
Cattle Drives – and Bill's Horses

Bill and his Partner Smoke

Smart Arab – Bill's horse Smoke

One day 19 years ago, our neighbor came knocking on our door. He was all excited and asked Bill if he would take the dumb Arab horse he had managed to bring to our house.

The horse was bleeding on one shoulder where a farrier had hit him with a mallet. He hit him because the horse wasn't cooperating when he was trying to shoe him. Of course that just made the horse more afraid and uncooperative.

The owner and the farrier became afraid of the horse and just wanted to get rid of him. The neighbor told Bill the horse was named Smoke and was a thoroughbred Arab. He also had papers on him. He couldn't do anything with him and he would sell the horse to Bill for $300 and give Bill the papers. Of course this was a challenge for Bill as he is one of the original Horse Whisperers that has patience with animals and knew how to gentle horses.

Bill bought Smoke and immediately started trying to gentle him. The first few times Bill rode him he had to put a blind over Smoke's eyes when he mounted him. After mounting, Bill would remove the blind (usually his coat) and Smoke would prance around a bit and then start walking where Bill reined him. It took a month or two to gentle him and he soon responded to Bill with respect.

Smoke didn't like water and would jump over the smallest "crick" or puddle. If Bill got in a tight spot Smoke would just freeze until Bill could get out of the situation.

For example, one day Bill was in Bloody Basin out hunting for deer and riding Smoke. Bill hadn't tightened the cinch tight enough and the saddle started slipping off Smoke. The strap to Bill's gun was around the saddle horn and strapped Bill onto the saddle as it was slipping off.

Smoke froze, and Bill managed to unbuckle the saddle cinch and slowly fall to the ground. A lot of horses would get excited, start bucking or just start running and drag the rider possibly to his death.

Another time Bill and Billie were riding along Red Creek. They came to a place where they needed to get down into the dry creek to cross it. Billie was riding Smoke and tried to neck rein him to turn a sharp left. She should have nose reined him so he knew what she wanted for sure. There was a three foot bluff on the right side of the creek and Smoke decided to go up it with a huge jump. Doing this he sucked in his belly and the saddle proceeded to slip off to the side and down went Billie to the ground. Smoke just stood there looking down at Billie like, "What are you doing down there?" Most horses would have stampeded and tore the saddle to pieces.

The first time we found out how smart Smoke was Bill had snuck a birthday cake out to Horse Camp for Billie's birthday. Billie wanted a picture of herself, the cake, and a horse. She was approaching another horse that didn't want anything to do with it. Smoke was eating hay in the horse trailer. When he saw what was going on, he came out of the trailer, put his head on Billie's shoulder and just stood there while our son Ben figured out how to work the camera to take the picture. Billie then told Smoke they were through. Smoke turned around and just went back into the horse trailer and started eating hay again.

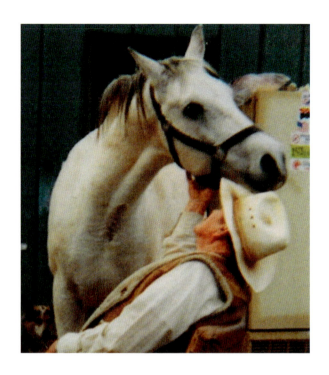

Bill and Smoke having fun at Horse Camp

We had a mustang named Chico that had been abused in his early life. Our son Billy had acquired him, and when the horse bucked Billy's daughter off, hurting her, Billy brought the horse to Bill. Bill worked with Chico for a number of months. Chico wanted to trust people in the worst way, but just couldn't. One day he would act gentle, and the next he wouldn't.

Bill took Chico to Horse Camp and turned him loose in the seven-acre fenced pasture there. Chico immediately turned wild mustang again and wouldn't even come to eat until no one was around. Bill then took Smoke up to the place Chico was and thought when he fed Smoke the next morning, Chico would come too and Bill would slip a rope on him. That didn't work either as Chico would come close, but not close enough. Bill decided to just leave him be and went back to the Horse Camp cabin.

That night Bill and Billie were playing cards before bedtime when there was a noise outside. They looked up and there was Smoke looking in the window, nodding his head, like come on out here. Bill opened the door to look out and there was Chico in the corral. Smoke had brought him in and was signaling Bill to go close the gate. The two horses could have come in, drank or ate, and went right back out to the pasture area.

Over the years, Bill enjoyed riding Smoke in the Fort Verde Parade in Camp Verde. Smoke would arch his neck and prance like Arabs do and make Bill proud to be his owner. One year, Bill carried one crutch to show one is never too old to ride. The crutch didn't bother Smoke and it came in handy at the end of the parade when Bill had to walk back up the street to be picked up.

Some people probably think these stories are made up, but they really happened. Smoke is almost 20 years old now. Bill still has Smoke and he will always be part of the Helm family.

2005 Bill riding Patchie and carrying "Wild Horse and Burro Association" entry flag in Fort Verde Days Parade

Bill breaking a horse at Willow Valley

Cattle Drives

Cattle Drive with cowboy in background

Cowboys pushing cattle

Billie Helm's shadow displayed while riding "drag" on cattle drive

Bill at brandin' time

Cattle being driven through Horse Camp
in the 1940's

Cattle roundup - roping, dehorning, castrating,
branding, and vaccinating

Billie Helm during Roundup

Chapter 6
Bill's Gold Stories

Is there really gold in "Bloody Basin" in Yavapai County, Arizona?

Bag of gold found at Wet Bottom Canyon by Mexican Sheepherder Chaparrals!

Our family went on a picnic one day at Tonto Basin. My brother George and my Dad began talking to a man that was camped beside us. He said he owned an auto court in Mesa. He asked them if they knew where Wet Bottom Canyon was in the Mazatzals.

He went on to say that some Mexican sheepherder chaparrals had been staying at his place in the fall. They had a pasture for their sheep in Mesa. In the summer, they had run their sheep in the Wet Bottom Canyon area along the Verde River.

This man showed my brother and dad a bottle filled with gold he had bought from these chaparrals. He said they were going to take him into Wet Bottom but they were taken back to Mexico by authorities before they could take him. So this man was lookin' for gold on his own.

George and Dad didn't know where Wet Bottom Canyon was but I did because I had run cattle off the Verde River when I worked for the Randall Ranch at the Verde Hot Springs.

Later on, Dad and I took some pack horses from the Randalls' ranch and went down the Verde River along the foot of the Mazatzals to where the Wet Bottom Canyon runs into the Verde River. One could ride a horse up the river into Wet Bottom Canyon. We wanted to see if we could find any gold.

We camped and stayed all night there. The next morning I told Dad I would do up the camp and take care of the horses and he could go on up the Canyon a foot and start pickin'. I also told him I would be up the Canyon from him with another camp set up.

I packed up and went back up the trail towards where we came down. I found the upper trail seven miles up the rim of the Canyon and dropped down to the bottom. I set up camp and waited for Dad to show up.

It was getting late in the evening and I got worried about my dad coming up that old rough rocky canyon a foot. I couldn't get a horse down it cause it was like a big granite wall. So I took off a foot as I already had the camp all made at the top of the Canyon and the horses taken care of.

Down the crick about a half mile through the rough and big rocks, and I could hear my Dad down there pickin' with his cross pick. I had also told him, "You watch for rattlesnakes, there's a lot of 'em in here." When I got to him I said, "Let's get out of here before it gets dark cause there's no trail going up the Wet Bottom." So we started out, it started getting' a little late, and there was a big ole' rattler right there by my Dad. He hit him with his cross pick and killed him. We made it on out to camp.

The next morning we took it a foot and we went up the Canyon with just a pick and gold pan. We stayed half a day up the Canyon and never found a bit of gold. When we came back to our camp, a bear had come down the trail into our camp and scattered our flour, sugar, and stuff all over. We stayed there that night, then my Dad said, "Bill, I think we'd better get out of here, I don't think we're goin' to find any gold." So next morning we packed up and got out of there.

My Dad told me this gold story

About 1925, Charlie and Ed Rosenberg were herding 17 head of cattle from Mayer through Dugas to the MT Ranch on the old freight wagon rim road.

Wagons full of supplies used to come from Mayer to Childs along this road. The two cowboys stopped the herd at the Verde River rim. They could see the MT Ranch from there and thought they might be able to find a shortcut through the canyon.

Charlie went down off the rim to find a shortcut. The canyon rim was just too brushy to take any cattle down. To Charlie's surprise he spotted an old "Spanish Raster" in the side of the canyon rim and went over to it. He found a lot of quartz rock with gold running through it in the bed of the raster. He took some of the rock up to the rim. He spent the night on the rim and took the cattle on down the old freight wagon road the next morning.

My Dad and Mom lived at the power company's Cedar Shack on the road near Childs. Dad was their trouble shooter at the time. The cattle drive stopped at their place and Charlie showed my Dad the quartz and gold rock and told Dad the he and his brother Ed were planning to go back there and retrieve some more of this rock after they got back to Mayer.

I was with my Dad later when he saw Charlie at Mayer and asked him if he ever went back there. Charlie said, "Don't put off till tomorrow what you can do today." Apparently he was still putting it off till tomorrow.

Spanish Gold Raster

I don't know if anybody knows what an old Spanish raster is but there is one in a side canyon where the Spanish found quartz with gold running through it. They used the raster to crush the rock they found.

Gold in Mazatzal Canyon down from Moonlight Mesa

There's another story told by ole' Grandpa Randall, an ole' original Mormon that came into Strawberry and Pine from Salt Lake City, Utah. Walt Randall (W. J. Randall) was his name. Their family had been there three or four years and had their roots pretty well planted. The old mail trail came through there and a couple guys came in there a foot. They were hungry and tired.

It was a rainin' and the ole' Mormons gave them a place to stay. They stayed at Pine a couple of weeks. These guys worked for 'em doing odd jobs like buildin' fence, cuttin' hay, and cleanin' horse corrals. So they woke up one bright and early morning and these guys were gone and had taken all the loose horses they could find in the night. They were headed for Phoenix evidently.

Grandpa Walt Randall's Dad, the Hunts, the Fullers, and the Randalls gathered up a few work horses they could find around Strawberry so they could trail these guys. Walt Randall said he was just a kid and he went with them. It was snowing and raining the next day.

They crossed the East Verde and up into the Mazatzals, that lower country, and came back up on a place they call Moonlight Mesa. I've never been there but always wanted to go there too. But according to Walt Randall, they found where the guys had camped on Moonlight Mesa.

The horses were just grazin' around up there and they found the guy's tracks where they had gone down the bottom of this canyon. They heard them down the canyon raisin' heck and they surrounded and captured 'em. It had been rainin', snowin', and sleetin' and down in the ripples of the water according to Grandpa Walt Randall they could see sparkly things that were gold nuggets.

The horse thieves were gathering them up. The Mormons weren't interested in the gold as they were farmers. I think the Fullers took the guys on into Payson. The two guys were hung for horse stealin'.

Walt and his Dad took the other horses back into Strawberry. When Grandpa Walt Randall was sittin' at the table tellin' this story I wanted to go in there lookin' but I never did. He claimed there were quite a few gold nuggets where they captured these guys. As far as I know, it is a true story, Grandpa Walt Randall wasn't the kind of person to tell a lie.

Is there gold in Monroe Canyon?

When I was a kid, the Randalls put me down on the Verde Hot Springs Ranch. There was no roads to there at all. There was no cabin at Horse Camp Canyon just an old tin shack down below Childs about 20 by 10. We kept supplies down there, coffee, and all kinds of dried beans, and grocery stuff.

That was the shack that was later dismantled and brought into Horse Camp Canyon. My job was packin' salt into Red Creek. I'd go over to the Hot Springs Ranch, pack three horses with blocks of salt, one horse with supplies and head for Horse Camp. On the way, I'd drop two salt blocks at Long Mesa.

Next day, I'd leave 2 blocks at Horse Camp and go to Red Creek where I left the rest of the salt blocks. I also took salt to Mockin' Bird Springs, Soda Springs, and Monroe Canyon when Lonnie Howard brought salt blocks by truck to Red Creek.

There was an old pipe line down there by the Red Creek Cabin. It ran down about one-half a mile and in the winter time the low places would freeze and bust. During the winter time I came down to the Red Creek Cabin up from the LX Bars horseback to fix the pipeline. There was an old road at this time but you couldn't drive up to Red Creek on it. The old foundation of the Cabin is still up there.

It was stormin' and rainin' and snowin' along the rim of Pine Mountain and the water was runnin' everyplace in all these canyons. So I went on in to the Verde River to another cabin that we kept some supplies in. I was cold and wet and I had three pack horses. As I came off Houston Creek Trail, I could see smoke comin' out of the chimney of the cabin. I rode on down there and unpacked the horses. When I went into the cabin an old hermit was in there.

All across Long Mesa and comin' down across the flats I could see where a guy'd been afoot goin' along the old trail. There he was in the old cabin. He had some coffee made and had the cabin all dirty. I kept a pretty clean cabin. He was cookin'. I had some old potatoes and stuff I had left there. They'd keep a month or two during the wintertime as long as you kept them from freezin'.

Anyway, he had them cooked up and I was mad when I saw he'd drank all my coffee. He said he was called Bradshaw. I asked him how he was goin' to pay for this coffee and all this chuck stuff he'd ate up. I told him, "It really makes it difficult when a guy comes in expecting to find wood for a nice warm cabin he can cook in."

He said, "Well, I'll pay yuh, I'll work for yuh." I said, "Well alright, I said we're goin' to chop some trail up there." It was still stormin' and rainin' and I couldn't get across the Verde River to the Hot Springs Ranch House cause the River was up. I thought in a couple of days it would be down and I needed to chop that trail out anyway. So I had a couple old axes and we chopped the trail up along the fence. We stayed a couple of days until the River'd gone down.

I had an old shotgun, an old Spencer. Every time we'd go out hunting in the fall it would fall apart. You had to put it back together to put a shell in it. You couldn't shoot it twice so you'd better make sure the first shot was good cause you'd have to dig the shell out and put another one in.

Anyhow, I went up the trail and killed a rabbit and a quail and brought them in and we cooked 'em. He said, "That's just what I need, and old shotgun." When I was getting ready to leave he said, "What would you take for it." I said, "This old shotgun ain't for sell, you couldn't pay for it anyway."

Then the old devil dug out a Bull Durham bag out of his pocket and dumped me out some gold on the table. I stood there and looked at it as I was sorta dumbfounded. I couldn't believe it was gold and picked some up and looked at it.

He said, "If that ain't enough," and dumped me out some more. I said, "Well, take that damn old shotgun." So he took it. I took this gold up to my Dad's at Irving and he said it was worth about $100 and somewhat dollars. That's when gold was about $30 an ounce.

There was one piece of gold that I'll never forget, it had a piece of white quartz on it. The gold was melted into the white quartz, a real pretty specimen. There's a lot of white quartz up in Monroe Canyon.

I asked old Bradshaw, "Where did you get that?" He said he didn't know the name of the canyon but I had seen his tracks in Monroe Canyon when I was up there. He said, "There was a spring of water comin' down this here little crevice. I could walk up it when it was rainin' and I could see holes. Down in the bottom of the little holes there was gold and I'd get it." Then he said, "I got hungry and cold so I came into this cabin."

To this day, I've never seen old Bradshaw again but that was real gold. I went up Monroe Canyon, took a gold pan and panned, and I looked and looked. I took two or three days up there lookin' and I never found any gold.

Another Gold Story

Bill Wingfield, Jr. (a cattle buyer that was going to buy the cattle from Randalls that year), and I were staying at Horse Camp Cabin right after the cabin was finished. He and I were ridin' up in the lower mountains between Yellow Jack and Red Creek. We'd been runnin' some cattle and our horses were winded pretty good. We were at the high point and George Randall and all the crew were waitin' down below.

We stopped there cause my saddle blanket was slippin' pretty bad on me off the back of my horse. So I took my saddle off and was straightening it up and Bill did the same thing. We aired our horses as they was weavin' and pretty sweaty.

I was puttin' my saddle back on when Bill said, "You know underneath this quartz ledge is some rusty stuff that could carry some gold, I'm goin' to take a piece with me." He was a pickin' around there so I took a piece of this rock and put it in my chap pocket. We went on and I sorta forgot about it.

I took it into Horse Camp and I put it up in the windowsill. One day I thought about my Dad always pannin' for gold so I decided to take that piece of rock into him at Irving. So I took it into the Hot Springs and finally got it up to Irving. He panned that rock for me and found a whole bunch of fine gold in it.

He said, "Come out here I want to show you something and he took that pan and whirled it around showed me the fine gold in the back of it." He said, "Do you know where that rock came from?" I said, "Yeah, I can go back to it." He said, "There's a rich deposit of gold in there."

Boy, I couldn't wait to get back over there. I built a bunch of location notices, some monuments and stuff, and I dug a hole there you could put a doggone car in. I'd pack that rock down and I'd hammer it up and never could get no gold out of it. I took some back into my Dad and he couldn't get gold out of it either.

Where that rock came from is such a natural formation one would think they could get gold out of it. The hole is still there.

Another Mysterious Gold Story

The old timers were always sittin' around telling stories. I was just a kid, I was the youngest one of the bunch and I didn't care much about gold. I cared more about wild cattle and what God created as I was sort of an old nature boy. Old Tuffy Peach and Hank Peach, I knew them real well, were chaparrals for the sheep outfit and they packed salt, groceries, clothing, and whatever was needed into the sheep camps.

Tuffy was also a cattle inspector, I guess, and he and Hank were wearing badges as they were regulating the sheep and cattle to keep another range war from happening. Anyway, they came into the old Kinsley Ranch one evening and as it was getting close to dark and they were asked to stay the night. They went up and ate and came back around the fire. There was a Mexican sheepherder herding goats there. He had a pile of rocks he was lookin' at with a light of some kind.

Old Tuffy Peach got to lookin' at this pile of rocks. There was a piece of quartz there that he broke open. The rock was just wired together with gold. He asked the Mexican where he got it and the reply was "No sabe." Kinsley said, "Yeh, he's herding those goats up around North Mountain." They kept trying to make the Mexican tell them what they wanted to know as they were excited about it. They told him they'd make it so he wouldn't have to work the rest of his life. But the Mexican just kept saying, "No sabe."

Kinsley did know a little Mexican, not much, and the sheepherder told him he would take them where he found the rock the next morning. They all went down for a good night's sleep and the next morning that Mexican was gone and they never saw him again. He probably didn't want them to know where he found the rock or the badges they were wearing scared him off.

Tuffy Peach and Mike Cullen – picture taken in 1962

Chapter 7
Bill Helm - House Builder and Trucker

House Builder and Carpenter

The house that Bill built

Bill's house built on Rocking Chair Road

The house that Bill built – while under construction

"Rocking Chair Road" House – Finished

This house was demolished when a bypass road was built that would have gone right through the middle of the house. This bypass road is an extension of Mingus Avenue and runs between Cottonwood and Highway 89A to Sedona.

Bill Helm Trucker and Logger

**Line up of CTI Trucks at Clarkdale
1964-65 Timeframe**

In 1960, Bill started hauling cement to the Glen Canyon Dam Project near Page, Arizona, for Belyea Trucking out of Cottonwood, Arizona. He delivered the 17th load of cement to the Dam. Bill also delivered the last load of cement to this Dam in 1964 driving for Cement Transporters, Inc, (CTI) out of Clarkdale, Arizona. When Bill arrived, he unloaded the truck he was driving (CTI #80), then he drove back over the bridge and was directed to pull into a big parking area where a celebration of this event was going on. When he got out of the truck he was greeted by the head of Merritt-Chapman & Scott Corporation that held the contract for the Dam. As they shook hands, the Arizona Republic newspaper took pictures and published the story.

Official construction of the Dam was started in 1956 with the first blast. Concrete placement started in 1957. This Dam tamed the waters of the Colorado River and created the 180-mile long Lake Powell along the

Utah/Arizona border. The Lake was named after John Wesley Powell. (Reclamation and Arizona, 2006)

Bill leased the Richfield bulk plant in Clarkdale from Atlantic Richfield. He also ran this service station in Cottonwood at the same time he drove truck for Belyea.

Bill Helm the trucker at Happy Jack

When there was little work on the ranches, Bill would go up to Flagstaff and work for Southwest Forest Industries. When there he would drive a logging truck and hauled logs. The place where the logging families lived was called "Happy Jack."

Top: Southwest Loggers
Bottom: Tony Sandoval and George Helm
Below: Gus Phillips (Bill's nephew)

Logging Trucks and a load of Logs

Bill lost the brakes on his logging truck one day, missed a curve, and ended up in the bottom of a canyon about 800 feet down. He did manage to ride the truck all the way down. He knew no one would find him for a long time so he managed to climb out of the canyon to get help. He only suffered minor injuries, which was a miracle.

Bill went to Alaska to work for the Alaskan Railroad for a short time. He also drove truck in Oregon for a while.

In the fall when Southwest shut down for the winter, he would go back down to the Randall Brothers' Ranch at Red Creek. After the roundup at Willow Valley in the spring, he would go back to Southwest for the summer. He did this for about 8 years.

Bill and truck he drove in Oregon

Bobby Parker and logging truck

Bill met Bobby Parker around 1956. Bobby was in his Army uniform and was visiting his parents in Flagstaff, Arizona. Bobby's parents' home was across the street from some other people that Bill knew and was visiting.

Later on Bill was working at a lumber camp named Happy Jack for Southwest Lumber Company out of Flagstaff, Arizona. Bill was driving logging trucks and Bobby was setting chokers. Chokers were set around logs then the logs were pulled through the chokers by a caterpillar (also called a skid cat). This procedure skid the bark off the logs. The logs were then loaded onto trucks with cranes. Some of the logs were 80-foot long. Bobby later drove logging trucks for many years also.

Bill and Bobby were good friends for many years. In later years, they really enjoyed getting together over a cup of coffee and sharing memories and stories.

When Bobby and his wife Marion moved to Camp Verde he had a workshop where he enjoyed making things out of horseshoes and other materials. He made Bill a hat and coat rack, name plate to put on his fireplace mantel with the name "Helm" on it. Bobby also decorated Bill's mail box with horseshoes.

Bobby was always ready to help a friend out. One day Bill's wife Billie called Bobby to ask if he would go with her to rescue Bill as he was broke down on the Bloody Basin road. Bill was pulling a horse trailer with several horses on his way home when the drive line fell out of his pickup. He was about 2 miles in from the I-17 freeway on a curvy, bumpy, dirt road. Anyway, it was a 25 mile trip one way. When Billie picked Bobby up he had a thermos of hot coffee ready to take to Bill.

When Bobby and Billie arrived where Bill was, Bill had a camp fire going, and offered Bobby a cup of coffee and a steak he had cooked. The horses were grazing around the camp.

Bobby hooked onto the horse trailer with his pickup. The horses were more than ready to get in the trailer for the trip home. Bill and Bobby went back later that day to bring his pickup home.

It was a sad day when Bobby passed away as a result of lung cancer at the age of 64.

Chapter 8
Irving Power Plant Reunion

Bill and long-time employee Cody Plante at Irving Plant Reunion in 2003

Company employee housing (2003 picture)

Irving power plant employee residences and commissary on the right

Bill and his Brother George at Irving Plant Reunion - 2003

Bill Crose, Frank and Judy (Helm) Valentine, Barbara (Helm) Mills

Gathering Memories at 2003 Plant Reunion

Bud and Loretta Eoff, Cody Plante, Billie and Bill Helm, Bill Crose

Bud and Loretta Eoff

Harrington Turner and Family

Lyman Lewis

**Employee and Families Reunion - 2003
Billie Helm, Patsy McMenamin, Cody Plante, PT,
(Patsy's Granddaughter), Bill Helm, John Newberry,
Bob Justus, Bob Baer**

George Helm, and Bob Justus being interviewed by Don Decker

Bob Baer and Don Decker

Chapter 9
Bill as Sheriff and Lawman

Bill's Deputy Sheriff Patch

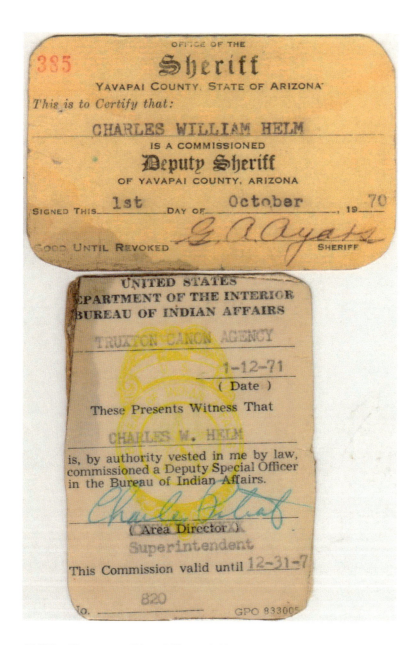

Bill's Deputy Sheriff and Deputy Special Officer
Bureau of Indian Affairs Identification

Bill's Deputy Sheriff Identification

Bill in his Cottonwood, AZ police department uniform with his Father George

During this time, Bill drove an old Chevy patrol car that went slow and smoked all of the time.

Walt Sanders, Frank Valentine, Ernie Medley, Dick Shipley, Steve Sharp, Bill Helm, Gil Melendez

Justice Court and Police Station in Cottonwood, AZ

Bill joined the Yavapai County Sheriff's Department and Coconino County Sheriff's Department in 1965 as a Deputy Sheriff and Sergeant for several years and retired in 1978. He was Chief of Police in Jerome for about two years. During that time, he was also a commissioned officer for the Bureau of Indian Affairs.

He was good at getting information from youngsters when he needed to solve a case that they were involved in. One of his ways of dealing with the youngsters was telling them about what he had done as a kid and then going on into the seriousness of some activities, even though they may have only been pranks.

Many in Camp Verde will remember when the Black Bridge north of town was taken down and replaced with a shining new concrete bridge. The sign which hung at the top of the old bridge disappeared. Bill remembers how he went about recovering the sign.

He put out the word that he was only interested in retrieving the sign. It wasn't long before one young man told him he knew where the sign was. Bill took him down to Childs and there was the sign hidden among some bushes. That sign with the date 1911 is now at the Hance House headquarters of the Camp Verde Historical Society. (Dickinson, 1991)

Bill remembers assisting with the removal of a whole group of squatters, including hippies, nudists, and possibly a fugitive or two, from the Verde Hot Springs area just above the power plant at Childs.

Bill Helm with Yavapai County Badge

Jail Break in Camp Verde

Chapter 10
Bill and Billie
Family and Friends

**Bill and Billie – Wedding Day Picture
October 1991**

Bill and Billie

Bill and Billie

Taken in Newman Cabin at "Pioneer Living History Museum" near Phoenix, Arizona

Bill and Billie at Cowboy Poetry Gathering at Sharlot Hall in Prescott, AZ

Bill and his brother George - taken at Willow Valley

Billie (Owens) Helm in the center with her children Sandra, Jonathan, Benjamin, Frank Jr., Pamela, Ginger

Marie Renee Helm, Randy Lee Helm, Judith Ann (Helm) Valentine, Charles William Helm, Jr., Bill Helm Sr.

Bill and Billy riding on Long Mesa in later years

Bill's daughter Judy (third from left) and Jeff, Terry (her daughter), and Daniel (her son)

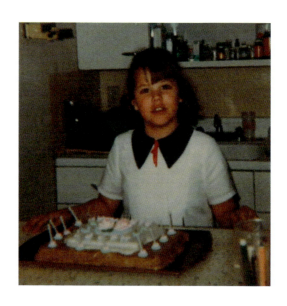

Bill's daughter Marie on her 10th Birthday

Marie at a very early age – all dressed up for Hollywood

Families that lived in the Fossil Creek Area

Some families that lived at Irving, Childs, and the Sally May house were: Newberry, Helm, Gerken (Owens), Vanderhoef, Eoff, Womack, Garrison, Godard, Hubbs, Robertson, Gunderlach, and Burris. Native American families that lived there and also worked on the flume were the Dixen Lewis family, the Turner family, and Jack Francis Family.

Bill's brother George and his family lived in a 3 bedroom house at Fossil Springs for 2 to 3 years. They moved to Childs when their children were old enough to go to school. George was the Chief Operator at Childs at that time.

At one time, their family lived at Stehr Lake. George caught and sold salamanders (water dogs) at the local lakes as he was not employed at the time. When water dogs turn into salamanders they can travel on land from tank to tank where there is more water to lay eggs.

One time Bill Helm told Ethel Godard he would catch the catfish in the tank near her home if she would cook them. She laughed and told Bill there weren't any catfish in that tank as they were water dogs.

Other families also raised gardens and would exchange fruit and vegetables and clothes in order to provide for their children.

Life was hard, but if a person was to talk to any of those pioneers they would tell you that the memories are happy ones and ones that are dear to their hearts.

Dixon Lewis Family

Bill on right with Bill Crose and Jackie Newberry on Bill Crose's Birthday

Longtime friends Charlie and Sue Franquero

Buckaroo Bill
By Clint Self

Buckaroo Bill was a good ranch hand,
Well acquainted with ouches and groans.
He earned his keep like cowboys do
Breaking horses and mules and bones.

He mended fences and packed out salt
And tended the cattle each day.
In the big Bloody Basin where cactus grows
And the Verde winds its way.

All the way down to the old sheep bridge
And north to the Verde Hot Springs,
Out where the coyotes howl at night,
There where the mocking bird sings.

The range was rough and life was tough
But Buckaroo Bill was too,
He took his turn at the Cowboy's life
Because that's what he loved to do.

Now Buckaroo Bill is gettin' old
Like another old man I know,
It's gettin' harder to stand up straight
And we walk around real slow.

Yet, he often longs for the old ranch life
And to hear the cattle bawl,
Down in the Basin where the filaree grows
And the mountains stand so tall.

Old Memories of Bloody Basin
By Charles (Bill) Helm

All an old man has of a long time ago are his memories.

I sit here thinking of all the good times. They were the best years of my life. I look off at the clear blue skies as far as I can see and it looks free to me. I could look off across the grand ridges, see cattle grazing and little calves bawling for their mothers. I could look out at the cattle and see the ones that needed my help. Sometimes I had to rope them and doctor them. Sometimes I had to brand a calf or two that we missed during roundup.

After the cowboys left to go to their homes, I was left behind to do my job packing salt, digging out water holes, building fences, and whatever else needed done. A cowboy's work was never done. My boss was a good man and so was the roundup crew. I was happy doing my job and that's why I love coming back to what I called my home at Horse Camp.

As I sit here at Horse Camp today, I don't see my cattle grazing on the ridges. All the old cowboys are dead and gone and I'm just about the only one left. I can still hear the cowboys coming off the ridges yelling at the cattle to get them into the pastures for the long drive. I'm sitting here thinking my memories are all I have left, I can't walk, can't hear well, but I can still see a little.

So I will do the best I can just holding on to the memories of what it was like in the good old days.

When I ride into the sunset, I want my ashes scattered there (Horse Camp) so that my spirit can still be wild and free.

If you were to ask Bill what he found most satisfying during his varied careers, he would tell you, after pondering a moment, "Cattle and ranch work and working with kids". As Bill puts it, "I've always got along real fine with the youngsters, just about as well as I got along with cattle, my horses, and my mule."

My Ole' Cowboy
Written about Bill Helm by Billie J. Helm
Copyright 2006

My ole' cowboy remembers cowboyin' somewhat
Different than some of these modern ways.
He likes to remember and
Talk about the "good ole days."

In central Arizona on the open range he herded the
Wild cattle, branded and dehorned them by himself.
He always had a running iron and dehorning
Saw on the back of his saddle.

Pay was one dollar a day, board was flour, water, beans,
Bacon, eggs, and sometimes a deer or a rabbit or two.

Room was on the ground under the stars at night
And in the morning - feeling the early dew.

My ole' cowboy liked being part of the cowhand team,
Playing' cards in the evenin' to see who did the cookin' and the
Night watchin', taking turns at point and drag on the cattle drive,
And pushin' the little doggies along so they would stay alive.

My ole' cowboy shod, broke, and doctored
His own horses for which he received no pay.
Later on, he helped build and clean the cabin at
"Horse Camp" where sometimes he would stay.

My ole' cowboy's way of fixin' things one really
Must admire. He's really skilled at using a plier.
It's amazing what he can fix with just
A piece of wire.

My ole' cowboy is known for his horse "smoke,"
Dog, "hobo," horse trailers with broken springs,
Dented four-wheel-drive red pickup, worn boots,
Spurs, chaps, western shirts with barbed
Wire holes, dusty hat, and worn out jeans.

Now, my ole' cowboy walks somewhat
Bent over, arthritis makes him sore,
Bowlegged from long days in the saddle
And he still wants to ride some more.

Look at my old cowboy's hands
With their calluses, scars, and lines.
Years of work and struggle
Have left their marks behind.

My ole' cowboy's face shows wear and worry,
His voice is soft and caring, his eyes are stern
But kind, and in his hair – wisdom in the form
Of silver threads you will find.

My ole' cowboy thanks his Maker for His creations,
The sun, moon and stars, flowers and trees,
Rain and the rainbow, wildlife, birds and bees.
He enjoys them every day and he asks God
For protection and guidance in his own way.

My ole' cowboy knows who he is, lives life simple,
And just keeps on a goin' even when he's
In a lot of pain. The good deeds he's done for
Others are remembered with his name.

My ole' cowboy has sparkling eyes, a great
Sense of humor, and a funny mischievous smile.
I'm prayin' God will continue to let him ride the
Trail of life for a long while.

Ole' Cowboy riding Cinnamon

Bill is an American Treasure, a hero that will never be forgotten in Arizona folklore and history. It won't be the same on the range when he "rides off into the sunset."

Billie Helm
Author of Pioneer Cowboy Bill Helm

About the Author

Billie Jean Crose Owens-Helm was born in Prescott, Arizona, in 1941. Her family came to Clarkdale in the Verde Valley when she was three. Her father worked for the Phelps Dodge Smelter Company during his career and retired from the Town of Clarkdale.

Billie's mother worked for the Clarkdale Post Office for many years. Billie was raised and attended kindergarten through high school in Clarkdale. She was a bookkeeper and teller for the First National Bank of Arizona right out of High School.

Billie is the mother of six children, has four stepchildren, and several grandchildren and great-grandchildren. She has lived all of her life in Arizona except for 14 years in Layton, Utah.

While in Utah she was a stay at home mom for seventeen years until finances forced her to seek employment. She was fortunate to gain employment with the USDA Forest Service Regional Information Office in Ogden, Utah.

When her husband Frank Owens' Pacific Intermountain Express truck driving job opened a relay station in Flagstaff, Arizona, his job change provided her the opportunity of a transfer. She transferred to the USDA Forest Service Supervisor's office in Flagstaff. Flagstaff is just 50 miles north of the Verde Valley where she grew up.

Five years later she was hired by the National Park Service at Montezuma Castle/Montezuma Well/Tuzigoot National Monuments in Camp Verde, Arizona, where she worked in the Administration Office for 15 years.

Billie marvels about how she was paid to move back home near her dad and other family members. This was especially important to her when Frank Owens, the father of her children, suddenly passed away at the age of 49.

She lived at Tuzigoot National Monument in park housing near Clarkdale for the next five years. She never dreamed she would live and work where she loved to hike and play as a child growing up. Her children then attended the schools she had gone to and some of their teachers were her classmates previously.

In October 1991, Billie married Charles William (Bill) Helm Sr. They moved to Camp Verde in 1992. In 2001 she transferred to the Albright Training Center at the Grand

Canyon and commuted to Camp Verde on weekends during her last two working years.

She now resides in Camp Verde with her husband Bill Helm, after retiring with 21 years of government service. She and her husband Bill have a small ranch where they have raised cattle and gentled wild horses. They still have two horses, one cow, a dog named Hobo, and several chickens.

Billie's purpose in creating and writing this book is to preserve the history of her cowboy husband Bill's life, and the places he and other settlers lived in surrounding areas. She is thankful to have pictures of historical places and structures that have since been torn down.

She also has pictures and some history of the people that built and lived at these places. Billie's purpose in composing her poetry and songs is to preserve the history of herself and her cowboy husband Bill, and their pioneer and present family. Billie also shares what it was really like growing up in early central Arizona along with her feelings, experiences, and her perception of life as she has lived it.

Some of Billie's uncles and great-uncles were the first cowboys in the Verde Valley in the early 1900's. Her husband Bill and these uncles are examples of what cowboys truly were and are like, stewards of the land and love for their country and families. She tells about this in her poem "The Real Cowboy of the West," on her CD. Billie's home and heart is in Arizona. Her CD called "Arizona Girl" can be purchased by calling 928-567-3108.

References

Schubert, Paul (1958, February 15) Round Up in Bloody Basin. *Saturday Evening Post*, pages 36, 37, 102, 104.

Arizona Public Service. *Childs-Irving: a History* [brochure].

Dickinson, Florence. (1991, November 29) Arizona from the Boots Ups: Helm Recalls Early Days of Verde Valley Law Enforcement. *Bugle* (Camp Verde edition of the Verde Independent).

Reclamation and Arizona. (2006) Glen Canyon Dam Completed!, 1960's, p. 1, 2, 3.
www.usbr.gov/lc/phoenix/AZ100/1960/topstory.html

Made in the USA
Charleston, SC
30 March 2015